TV News Channels in India

Published by
ACADEMIC FOUNDATION
in association with

CMS™
www.cmsindia.org

TV News Channels in India

Business, Content & Regulation

Edited by

P.N. Vasanti

Prabhakar Kumar

ACADEMIC FOUNDATION

NEW DELHI

www.academicfoundation.com

First published in 2016
by

ACADEMIC FOUNDATION
4772-73 / 23 Bharat Ram Road, (23 Ansari Road),
Darya Ganj, New Delhi - 110 002 (India).
Phones : 23245001 / 02 / 03 / 04.
Fax : +91-11-23245005.
E-mail : books@academicfoundation.com
www.academicfoundation.com

Disclaimer:
The findings/views/opinions expressed in this book are solely those of the authors and do not necessarily reflect the views of the publisher.

Cataloging in Publication Data--DK
Courtesy: D.K. Agencies (P) Ltd. <docinfo@dkagencies.com>

TV news channels in India : business, content & regulation /
edited by P.N. Vasanti, Prabhakar Kumar.
pages cm
Contributed articles.
ISBN 9789332703254

1. Television broadcasting of news--India. 2. Television--Law and legislation--India. I. Vasanti, P. N., editor. II. Kumar, Prabhakar, editor.

PN5377.T4T86 2016 DDC 070.430954 23

Typeset by Italics India, New Delhi.

Printed and bound by The Book Mint, New Delhi.
www.thebookmint.in

CONTENTS

Section III
Regional Surge

Section IV
Content Format/Structure

Section V
Issues

List of Tables, Figures and Annexures

Tables

Figures

Annexures

About the Editors/Contributors

Editors:

P.N. Vasanti is Director-General of Centre for Media Studies (CMS). She is a researcher and specialist in studies on media habits, policy issues in broadcasting and media consumption patterns. Her concerns include: the impact and role of media; use and implications of various communication forms on behaviour/practice. She is also an independent adviser on research, policy and strategies in communication and media sector.

Prabhakar Kumar is Head of CMS Media Lab. He has over 13 years of experience in media research, production and training. He has led the research projects on prime-time TV news programmes of 90,000 hours. He is a member of the Scrutiny Committee (on Violations) of Electronic Media Monitoring Centre (EMMC) under the Ministry of Information and Broadcasting since 2008. His area of research includes critical analysis of different domains of Indian media and its quality.

Contributors:

N. Bhaskara Rao is the founder and Chairman of CMS, New Delhi. He is a pioneer of social research in India and an eminent mass communication expert with almost 50 years of distinguished background. Dr Rao is an authority on media utilisation strategies and communication policies. He has been a member of high level standing Advisory Committee of Information and Broadcasting Ministry. He is author of a number of books on governance, media, elections and interstate politics.

Daya Kishan Thussu is Professor of International Communication and Co-Director of India Media Centre at the University of Westminster in London. Prof Thussu is the founder and Managing Editor of the Sage journal *Global Media and Communication*.

Geeta Seshu is a senior journalist and writes on free speech, women and representation and media ethics. She is Consulting Editor of the media watch site, *The Hoot*.

Anuradha Raman is associate editor of the *Hindu*. She engages on issues ranging from media to gender and education. Her past assignments include critical comments on policies of the government.

K.S. Arul Selvan has a decade-long experience in media training and research in national and international projects and institutions. His area of specialisation is New Media. He was heading the media department at the Tezpur Central University before joining IGNOU as Associate Professor.

Mrinal Talukdar is currently associated with DY365, where he runs a popular prime-time talk show. After spending nearly 20 years in print, including his long innings in UNI, he moved to television in 2010.

Shravan Garg has been a print media journalist with an experience spanning four decades. He previously worked with *Dainik Bhaskar* as Group Editor and *Nai Dunia* as Chief Editor.

Sonia Singh is Editorial Director and President of the NDTV Ethics Committee. She is an NDTV veteran and has been with the company since 1992. She was conferred with the "Young Leader Award" by FICCI.

N.K. Singh is General Secretary of Broadcast Editors' Association (BEA). He is a veteran journalist and has worked with print and electronic media.

Sudhir Rinten is Assistant Professor at Maharaja Agrasen College, University of Delhi. His main research area lies in the subject of politics, media and entertainment.

Alok Srivastava is Director, CMS Social—a social research team of CMS India. He has more than two decades of experience in social development research. His area of research work includes GCCM (governance, corruption, community and media).

Note from Editors

TV News Channels in India is the first book based on empirical data available through a decade long research on TV news content. There is a scarcity of data on different aspects/domains of TV media in India and whatever is available, lacks credibility as various sources paint different pictures whether it is related to ownership, business or content. The reasons are multiple. CMS visualised this more than 10 years ago and set up CMS Media Lab with a commitment to create a databank of TV news content to encourage informed discussion based on credible facts and figures. Our effort and vision to empower news media generated a statistical history of TV news content trends, based on nearly 90,000 hours of news programmes. We feel proud to fulfil our vision and commitment to provide reliable data in TV news content even without any external grant or fund.

The journey of content analysis of TV news channels started in 2005. We analysed the trends in the coverage of TV news on the basis of time spent on issues every day in these news programmes. The trends are based on the prime time (7-11PM IST) coverage of six TV news channels—Aaj Tak, ABP News, Zee News, DD News, Sahara Samay and NDTV India (all five are in Hindi except DD News which is bilingual). In 2008, the two Hindi news channels, Sahara Samay and NDTV India, were replaced with English channels—CNN-IBN and NDTV 24x7. The change was made to gauze the English news channels' trends as well. This has continued till 2014.

Availability of such rich time-series data motivated us to bring out the present book and enrich the discussions towards further improving television news content. However, we wanted to include other equally relevant and complementing issues in the book. Besides content, ownership, business and regulation of TV news in India were also included. To have voices of different stakeholders, perspectives of industry experts, professors, editors and researchers were invited to contribute to this publication.

For easy reading and focus on critical components of television news channels, the book is divided into five sections. The first section, Overview, provides the existing scenario of TV news where N. Bhaskara Rao has highlighted the Indian picture, while Daya Thussu presents it from the perspective of an international viewer of Indian news channels.

The second section is on Policy and Regulation, wherein Geeta Seshu has contributed a chapter on television and regulation based on extensive research of media policies. Anuradha Raman, in this section, has highlighted critical and crucial issues related to ownership of TV news channels.

The third section—Regional Surge is a compilation of commentary on south Indian TV news scene by Arul Selvan and TV news scene in north-east India by Mrinal Talukdar. They have provided information and analysis, which is hardly recorded and discussed in public domain.

Fourth section covering Content Format showcases the ideas and structural issues of TV news by three senior journalists—Sonia Singh, N.K. Singh and Shravan Garg. Shravan Garag has dealt with trivialisation of TV news content in India and painted the tragedies of prime time TV news, whereas N.K. Singh critically analysed the role of presenter in a discourse and commented on what an anchor should do through a story based on Amartya Sen's book, *The Idea of Justice*. Sonia Singh in her contribution commented on the structure of TV news content and analysed the reasons of increasing talking TV syndrome in news *versus* talk.

The fifth and last section deals with specific issues, entertainment and corruption, covered in TV news content in the last one decade. Sudhir Rinten explored the factors and tendency of TV news channels to 'entertainise' news programmes, whereas Alok Srivastava did micro scanning of the corruption coverage in TV with interesting case studies.

Further, to give the readers an opportunity to analyse the trends of TV news and get more insights, CMS Media Lab compiled data tables which are annexed. The book also contains an interesting exercise, developed by Alok Srivastava, for readers to gauge the television news channels.

We believe the perspectives of multiple authors would prove invaluable resource for observers of TV news channels in India.

— P.N. Vasanti and Prabhakar Kumar

1

N. BHASKARA RAO

The Scene of News Channels in India

The 1995-2015 period has witnessed unprecedented growth and changes in the Indian media scene—both qualitatively and quantitatively. This change happened because of the eagerness of news channels to reach out and cover the happenings competitively, faster and with field footage. The proliferation has been within and across mass media. There is no parallel in the world for this kind of dramatic spurt and change in the media scene. One of the significant structural changes is the emergence of television as a news media from being primarily an entertainment media until around 2000.

Against one Indian television channel (Doordarshan) with one or two TV news bulletins a day 25 years ago, there were 88 news channels in the country in 2005. But, by January 2015, that number has risen to 405 news channels, each with round the clock news in one form or other and half-hourly "news bulletins". Some non-news channels (general entertainment channels) too continue to give 2-3 news bulletins a day. Also, while the news scenario earlier was dominated by English language newspapers, it is the Indian language ones that continue to proliferate in this decade (including in the case of television). News channels are there in every major Indian languages (in 14 different languages). In fact, the growth and proliferation in television channels, particularly news channels, have come from regional languages. There are certain regions in South India, for example Andhra Pradesh and Kerala, where the number of news channels is as high as the number of GEC (general entertainment channels).

News channels received a huge audience boost by actively covering party politics, elections, political controversies and corruption and facilitating rational discourse and debate within the public sphere. The political uncertainty the country experienced in the last decade also contributed to television emerging as the 'primary source' of news in the country. The model being followed by these 24-hour news channels has been going through shifts in priorities and changes in their structure. The national news scene in the case of television is dominated by Delhi-based news channels, mostly in Hindi.

With over 161 million TV homes and well over 825 million (FICCI-KPMG Report 2014) viewers, the potential of 24-hour news channels is mind boggling in many contexts—political, social and, of course, the markets. However, the increase in TV news viewership is not proportionate to that in the number of news channels over the years.

Viewership of News Channels

The proliferation of channels did not significantly increase viewership between 2006 and 2013. The year 2008 marked a decline in news channel viewership when regional news channels saved the situation. Viewership to English news channels declined further in favour of increase in viewership of regional news channels. Even Hindi news channels did not add viewership.

Figure 1.1

Viewership of TV News Channels

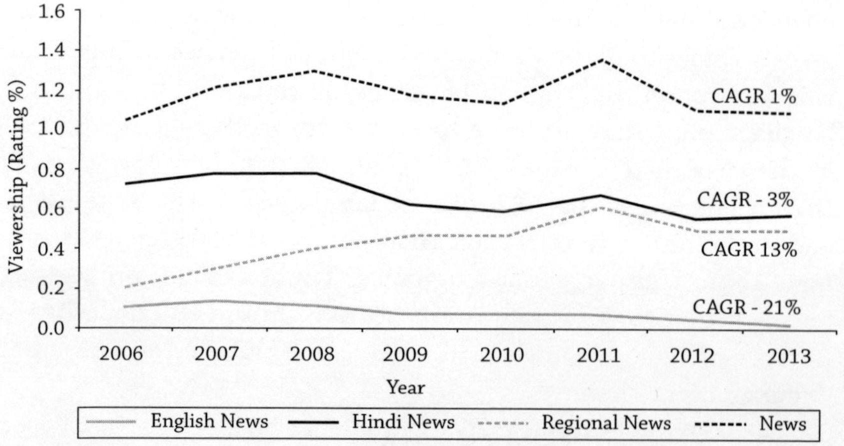

Source: NBA *Annual Report 2013-14*.

Emergence of Television as Primary News Media

Owing to round-the-clock news channels nationally and regionally across the country and their live coverage potential, television today has emerged as a primary source of news in India. Nevertheless, newspapers remain a serious and even more credible source of news, as tracking studies by CMS have brought out. Interestingly, these studies have also brought out the "appetizer effect" of news channels. That is, the one who watches news bulletins on TV, are more likely to read newspapers. It implies, contrary to general perceptions, that proliferation of news channels initially has helped newspapers to consolidate and grow both vertically and horizontally. This trend in the growth of newspapers has also been corroborated first in 2005 by two national surveys (National Readership Survey [NRS] and Indian Readership Survey [IRS]). Some increase in the circulation of newspapers and viewership of channels, nevertheless, is more because of multiplicity, as opposed to expansion of their reach. This implies that the ones watching TV are watching more channels or programmes, and the ones reading are reading more newspapers. No wonder, then, that multiplicity of news channels has not led to commensurate increased viewing of TV news nor has it led to any decline in reading daily newspapers, although there is a decline in the time spent for reading. Also, the duration of viewing news on TV on an average day has declined in metros. This trend was also indicated by viewership surveys.

Competition between media (newspapers and television) and within each of them (in-between various TV channels) has given boost to numbers, expanded the scope of media, opened up new vistas and the potential for further growth of mass media. However, the same thing cannot be said about the overall credibility of news media, commensurate to their proliferation. In fact, thanks to 24-hour news channels, credibility of newspapers has gone up, however, marginally. TV news channels, on the other hand, have not improved their credibility or commensurately increased overall reach or expanded, as one would expect. The increase was more sporadic in nature and not conducive to realise full potential.

However, TV news channels have now emerged as the primary source for news and current affairs, without eroding the importance of newspapers as it is happening in some countries. In the initial period, television news bulletins were guided more by the contents of newspapers, but of late, there has been a reversal of roles. Together, newspapers and news channels set the public agenda of the country—regionally and nationally—for politics, the Parliament, the government and even the markets. The contents of news media in some respects influence markets and reflect the mood of the nation, concerns of policymakers, priorities of the government of the day.

In their coverage, news channels are expected to expand the scope of news coverage and viewership of news bulletins, increase their pro-activeness and make a distinct difference. The four parameters in that regard are: origin of news; concern as evident from the subject matter of contents covered; extent of certain news reports, and scope of coverage as news or features; and participation or inclusiveness in reflecting the viewpoints or engaging people. To understand these trends over time, CMS Media Lab has been tracking news media every day for their contents and analysing them—for more than a decade. In the case of TV news, news bulletins of major 'national' channels are recorded every day, where contents are analysed by news analysts. Some of the highlights referred here are based on CMS Media Lab tracking.

Subject Categories of News Bulletins

Samples of News Channels

2005-2007: Aaj Tak, Sahara Samay, Star News, Zee News, NDTV India, DD News

2008-2014: Aaj Tak, DD News, ABP News/Star News, Zee News, CNN IBN, NDTV 24x7

Politics, sports, crime, law and order and markets—these five categories together, account for nearly two-third of news bulletin items of 24-hour news channels. Coverage of rural India by news channels has been a casual affair, as if just to remind viewers that they are 'national'. Even in terms of the subject matter of news

Figure 1.2

TV News Trends

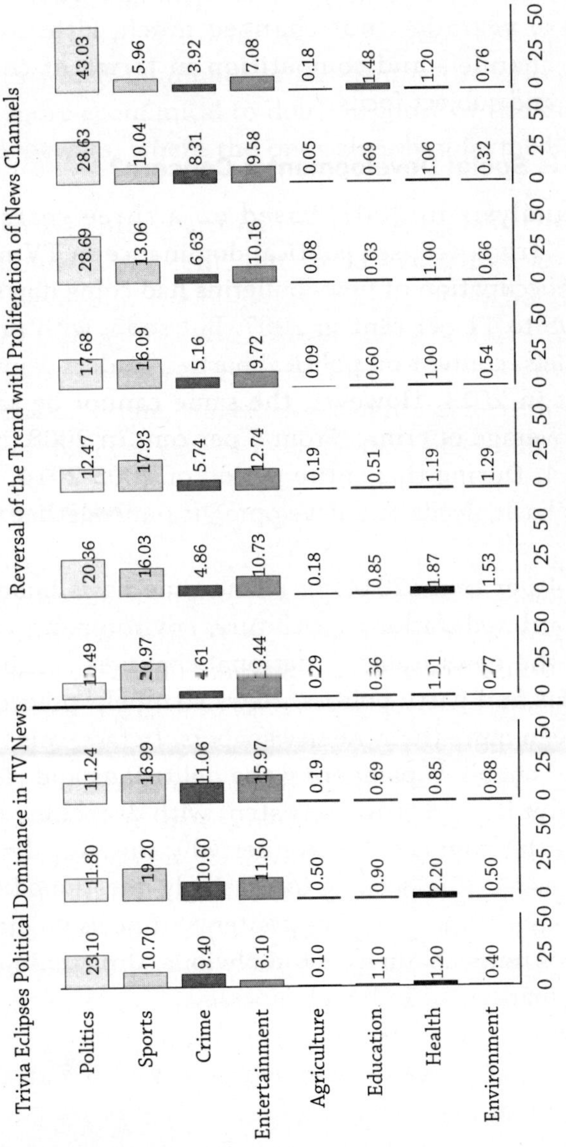

Source: CMS Media Lab.

Figure given below is only for 2003–2005 period to indicate the extent of repeats).

Figure 1.3

Repeat of Stories in Prime Time

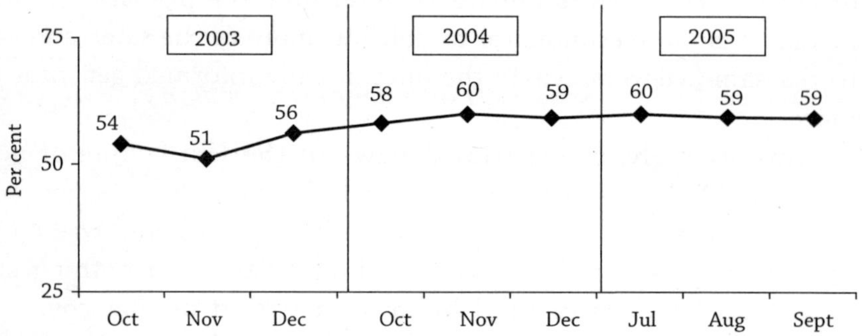

Source: CMS Media Lab.

However, it is the extensive repeat of the same news in the news bulletins of round-the-clock news channels that gives the impression that nothing more or else and as important is happening in the countryside and across. Limitations of TV (cost, logistics, time, technological) as a news medium are setting the criteria for what is news of the day and their priorities in the presentation of news bulletins are often misleading. Now, newspapers are trying to emulate and compete with TV news channels. News bulletins of neither of the national news channels, distinguish themselves as reflective of India. There is a dire need for more reflective news agenda for the country, which is more democratic, representative, inclusive, and catering to the 'felt needs' and peculiar socio-economic features of the country.

As one expert commented not very long ago, some news channels are converting themselves into crime (promoting) channels during late nights. In the process, news values and priorities are becoming more and more contentious, without any restraint on hyping and repeating gory visuals that have nothing to do with news of the day. Such a scenario calls for specific regulations, both from within and outside, including the government.

Box 1.1

New Experiments in Public Broadcasting in India

Lok Sabha TV (LSTV)

Lok Sabha TV was launched in 2006 by then Lok Sabha (Lower House of Parliament) Speaker Somnath Chatterjee. The idea of having a dedicated channel for the Lok Sabha took shape while Chatterjee felt the need to showcase good, bad and ugly part of elected representatives' behaviour in the Parliament to citizens of India. This idea got further momentum due to perennial neglect of Lok Sabha proceedings by mainstream media.

This channel runs opinion and feature based programmes including live proceedings of the Lok Sabha during sessions. It telecasts programmes on democracy, governance, social, politics, and constitution. Some important elements of this channel include: debates, discussions and documentaries on important social and political issues. The channel also telecasts some award winning films, some of which portray the historical significance of India. Before the launch of LSTV, proceedings of both houses used to be shown on DD Loksabha.

LSTV is not very popular like mainstream news channels, however, it has created its space among serious viewers.

Rajya Sabha TV (RSTV)

Rajya Sabha TV (RSTV) started its broadcasting on 26 August 2011, after the five years of launch of LSTV. It is a 24x7 Parliamentary TV channel which telecasts the proceedings and the activities of the Rajya Sabha (Upper House of the Parliament). The channel provides an in-depth coverage and analysis of topics which are discussed in the proceedings of the Rajya Sabha.

Apart from the live coverage of proceedings of Rajya Sabha, it presents deeper insights in the functioning of the Parliamentary processes. It also covers the aspects of social, political, economic and cultural life of the people.

RSTV has created a model for both private and public current affairs channels on how to serve the core purpose and raise the quality of information and opinion delivery while competing in wild entertaining and sensational news market. In the public and private broadcasting space, it also runs a weekly program on critical review of media behaviour.

Its programming structure is different from LSTV and shows national and International news. Unlike LSTV, it does not take private advertisements and fully dependent on the government grant.

Content Model of News Channels

Thus, overall, with the onset of 24x7 news channels more than a decade ago, the "news" contents have come down to less than half of the telecast time. The remaining telecast time in this model is being used for non-news contents; some of them in the garb of news and current affairs, and others having little to do with hard news of the day or week. This trend is significant, as it indicates that 24x7 channel idea may not be viable with a couple of news channels as an exception, unless Anna Hazare or Ram Dev or other such campaigns or agitations or political crisis sagas are on. This is somewhat the chicken and egg syndrome, where the kind of 'news' provided and the way in which it is provided are not attracting commensurately more viewers (despite being the primary source), and in a sustained way. As a result, commercial revenue of news channels is not increasing proportionately, and whatever allocations are there now have to be distributed between increasing number of news channels. This trend is already being realised, although it has not stopped more news channels being added.

Government Policies

There are no specific new (or old) regulations that have been made in the wake of proliferation of public and private news channels, except what has been provided in the Cable TV Network (Regulation) Act (1995), which are only broad guidelines that make no difference to actual operations or priorities of news bulletins. One of the guidelines is that there should be no derogatory coverage of countries friendly to India (as if there are no permanent friends or otherwise). Downlinking policy (November 2005) made it obligatory for channels to register in India and declare revenue and also pay a one-time fee to the government.

However, there have been periodic demands from political leaders for restraints on the news media when the coverage was not suitable for them. As if reflecting those demands, most Ministers taking up the Information and Broadcasting portfolio, hints at intentions of the government to come up with one or other kind of regulatory provision. This demand reached a new height in the wake of the Mumbai attack in 2009, when the coverage of news channels came under severe attack, thereby making the Minister of Information and Broadcasting to reiterate government's resolve to bring news channels under some regulations. Rising to the occasion, the big news channels took the initiative of forming an association of news channels, the News Broadcasters Association (NBA), and as a self-regulatory initiative, appointed a retired Supreme Court Judge and sought complaints from public. The complaint to this Authority, irrespective of how many news channels it represents, has to be accompanied initially with a fee of ₹1000. No wonder why hardly a couple of complaints were received in the first year or more. However, Justice J.S. Verma, who headed that Authority, took the proactive (*suo-motu*) initiatives of calling TV channels to explain certain objectionable coverage of news bulletins, and even imposed a fine and asked them to prominently mention the advice in the news bulletins.

The eventual and ultimate interest of TRP driven content model is to support, sustain, promote and perpetuate consumerism. Advertisers are no longer 'hidden persuaders' as they account for nearly 65 per cent of the revenue of channels. In fact, top 20 advertising agencies in India are foreign-owned/controlled.

Catering to the Interests of Advertisers

Mindshare is a leading advertising space buyer and it sponsors high-budget special programmes on TV channels. In an interview to *Business Standard* reporter (18 September 2012), Anita Kotwani, Principal Partner of Mindshare said,

> If the channel is *guaranteeing eyeballs for the committed outlays*, advertisers will not shy away from it (the programme). And, if the *brand is interweaved into the content*, with a perfect fit, as part of the outlay committed, it adds, as a sweetener to explore the property' (sponsored programme) (emphases added).

What does this mean? What is the message such contention sends out—to channels, to content producers—on content priorities and even on structure or format of the programmes. The intrusion into channel's prerogatives is directed by advertisement agencies and the implementation of their plan by way of TRPs (television rating points). This is what a Chief Executive Officer (CEO) of a Telugu news channel said (reading out the prescription from a TAM advice) at a CMS workshop (2005) on paradigm shift.

Figure 1.4

Advertisement Revenue of TV News Channels

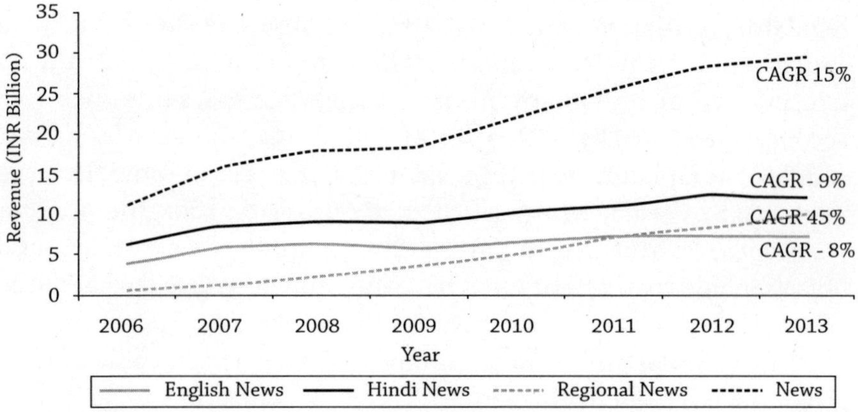

Source: NBA *Annual Report 2013-14*.

News channels are more interested in catering to the needs of advertisers and convenience of advertisement agencies as viewers are not seen as direct cause of revenue. Channels somehow are interested more in figuring favourably in TRPs so that they could get the support of advertising agencies. Their struggle to cope with competition leaves them unable to focus on bringing relevant programmes to the larger public and driving new initiatives on the programming front. All that however could be expected to change after complete digitalisation (that is already initiated). But if rating system of television remains same as now, I am afraid, it is not going to change the dependence on advertising as the primary source of revenue.

Three aspects of advertisements in the context of news channels also determine the scope and standing of news channels. First, since news channels are free-to-air (as of now), they depend primarily on advertising support for their survival and viability. A second consideration is the extent (number and frequency of breaks) of advertisements in news bulletins. Third, with full digitalisation of channels around the corner, news channels will become pay-for-view or pay channels. What are the pros and cons of that? What would be the government policy to ensure access to news to every one?

Table 1.1

Percentage of Advertisement Time in News Channels (2008-2011)

Year	*In per cent*
2008	34.0
2009	35.4
2010	35.6
2011	35.4

Source: TRAI Consultation Paper (No.7/2012).

Telecom Regulatory Authority of India (TRAI) issued a consultation paper (No.7/2012) on 16 March 2012 on 'issues related to advertisements in channels', including news channels. For that analysis, TRAI extensively used CMS Media Lab data. It issued its draft regulations on 28 August 2012. This analysis of advertising time in the news bulletins of news channels (six English and Hindi), brought out that the extent of advertisement has been on increase over the last few years. On an average, 35 per cent of prime time of the news bulletins is commercials against 20 per cent limit prescribed in the existing regulation. In fact, the maximum yearly average according to TRAI's paper is as high as 47.4 per cent. Even the minimum has been going up from 14 to 23 per cent.

Apart from the duration of the advertisements, the other concern of TRAI from the perspective of the viewers' experience was the frequency of advertisements. The frequency as well as the timing of advertisements to a large extent determines their contribution to irritation at the viewer's end, (TRAI Consultation Paper, p.8). The other point that TRAI raised was the high audio level of advertisements even in news bulletins. Clutter of screen with advertisements even to the extent of missing the news or making it difficult to differentiate and comprehend news was indicated.

channel is the only channel which is operating as a separate channel 'for women'.

Despite proliferation of news media and competitiveness between news channels, the choice in the content package of news bulletins is not so distinct from one channel to another—in the case of both national and regional channels. Contents of the television channels, today, are based on certain misleading notions and formula adopted mostly on the basis of surrogate viewership yardsticks and as a reaction or in response to competitive compulsions. This practice, in many ways, has limited, restrained and constrained creative calibre and the genius of channels. This is also true in the case of news channels. This is not only with regards to the subject of contents, but also their scope, structure, schedule, formats and even participative aspects. Tinkering with marginal changes will not do anything for distinguishing news channels. All practices require a relook, a review and redesign. That is not possible without systematically 'disrupting' the present priorities, practices, schedules and systems of deciding the contents, programming patterns, etc. What is needed as an interim measure, before the channel starts distinguishing itself, is 'disruptive programming'. This involves doing differently with respect to time schedules, formats, subjects, participation, and even studio design, dress codes, and durations of various programmes (could be shorter or longer than at present), tagline, etc. A recent Gemini News channel's attempt to present Telugu news bulletins from outside studio, from a market or street corner is one such example (whether it has made a difference has to be talked by the channel).

Disruptive programming calls for more creative initiatives, quickness in execution and mounting programmes spontaneously from within the channel. The duration of such a period could be 6-12 months, during which period it should go for strategic research to facilitate and lead on to a new programming phase without losing viewers in the process.

Disruptive programming should lead to distinguish the channel from its competitors. Innovative initiatives have to be far more daring (full of risks!) and executed confidently, backed by promotion strategy. The ingenuity of channel operators (producers) should be evident. A good example for a channel to start disruptive move could be by way of redefining the very idea and practice of 'prime time'. The way the screen is used with bottom lines like 'breaking news' could be done in another way. Changing tagline or/and converting it into practice in programming and programme schedules is another type of disruptive programming.

Based on field research over the years, it is suggested that a 'needs based programming' is likely to work better and give better results in terms of viewership, impact and positioning of a channel in the long run. The needs-based strategy for a news channel consists of more 'entertainment-education-informative-empowerment' based contents (more specifically, this could be soft areas where television hitherto made hardly any difference). This broadly means programmes that empower viewers, activate them as citizens, discerning consumers, sensitise parents, etc. and build capacities to resolve conflicts locally. To make such a difference, one has to have a strategy and sustained efforts. In this process, there cannot be fixed formula or dos and don'ts that will work in every situation and for every channel. Things have to be dynamic with contents that have potential to lead and elevate viewers and people to higher levels of lifestyles, civic life, productive role, human relationships, etc.

This dilemma is more obvious in the case of TV channels than in print media. What induces or motivates people to watch a channel more than other? Obviously it is the interest that the content arises in the viewers.

Making a viewer interested to look at the screen, even if it is the same content that is being shown again and again, does not necessarily mean that it is also 'in the interest' of the viewer in the immediate context or otherwise. In fact, it happens in exceptional cases when a channel shows something that is 'interesting' to look at and is also 'in the interest' of the viewers, particularly to more viewers if not to as many viewers; and if not immediately, then at least, in the long run. Such content could be described as a 'win-win offer'.

The Indian civilisation has a tradition of communicating 'what is in the interest of people' through folk tales, epics, and all kinds of vocal culture and creative arts in an interesting and enthusing way. This model is described as the entertainment-education approach. Field research shows special sway towards such an approach. In fact, the leads for this approach have come from field research, not so much from TRPs. Such an entertainment-education approach requires relatively more field research and more enquiry in every aspect.

With proliferation of channels and keen competition among them, one cannot imagine contents and programme schedules without planning, strategy, research and innovation. Here, it is suggested that the need-based approach to contents, along with entertainment-education strategy, is more likely to distinguish the channel in a positive context. Needs orientation comes from concerns and that should become the driving force.

2

DAYA KISHAN THUSSU

The Voice of the Global South?

TV News from India

International television news has changed profoundly in the past two decades, reflecting the cumulative impact of liberalisation, privatisation and deregulation of the media and communication sector, together with the digitisation of content, enabling global and instantaneous circulation of television news across continents. While the imbalance in the flow of news—from the media-rich North (and within it a US-UK [United States-United Kingdom] core) to the South—continues to define global television news, in an era of multi-vocal, multi-layered and multi-directional flows, the traditional domination of Western, or specifically American, media is diminishing, and, more importantly and arguably, being challenged (Nordenstreng and Thussu, 2015). In a complex, globalised world, international news is in the process of transformation, partly as a result of an increasingly mobile and globally networked and digitised communication infrastructure, leading to availability of news from such diverse countries as Russia, China, India and Qatar. In this chapter, I focus on how Indian television news is aiming to reach a global audience. With more than 300 round-the-clock news channels and a strong tradition of English-language journalism, Indian perspectives on global affairs is accessible *via* such channels as News 18 India, part of the TV-18 group, as well as NDTV 24x7, part of New Delhi Television Group, which has been operating for a quarter of a century, providing quality news. Both are private networks, while the Indian state broadcaster Doordarshan (DD) remains one of the few major state news networks not available on television screens in key markets at a time when global television news in English has expanded to include inputs from countries where English is not widely used, including Japan and Iran.

In an era of visually-driven global geo-politics, the importance of television news in a country's external communication strategy cannot be overemphasised. Unlike other established and emerging powers, Indian presence in international news arena is characterised by private not public broadcasters. This is ironic, given India's traditional role in articulating Southern concerns in international forums—most notably during the 1970s NWICO (New World Information and Communication Order) debates within United Nations Educational, Scientific and Cultural Organisation (UNESCO), and more recently its emergence as an economic and political power. After providing a historical context to the evolution of India's television news, this chapter will suggest that, with more than 300 round-the-clock news channels and a well-established English-language journalism—the vehicle for transnational communication and commerce—Indian journalists are well able to operate in a global media sphere: Indian-born or Indian-origin journalists are visible in leading international news outlets. However, while the all-news channels in India are just over a decade in existence, even in their early formative years their pro-business agenda was well formed. Are Indian television channels the voice of the global South or an echo of a US-dominated market-driven broadcasting culture, hostage to Bollywoodised infotainment?

The global news sphere has been dominated by what has been called a 'US-UK news duopoly'—visible both in state-sponsored channels (such as the Voice of America and its associated global networks), and perhaps more effective, private television news with their formidable economic muscle. The US government-sponsored news initiatives have been supported by a thriving and globalised private news media—from television news agencies (Reuters Television and APTN) to international news networks (CNN International and CNBC, to name the prominent ones). One reason for the US domination of global media is that the country has always followed a commercial model for its media industry—a venture in which the successive US governments have been a crucial factor. Broadcasting—both radio and television—had a commercial remit from its very inception. The commercially-driven trio of networks—Columbia Broadcasting System (CBS), National Broadcasting Corporation (NBC) and American Broadcasting Corporation (ABC)—provided both mass entertainment and public information. In the post-Cold War world, the US-inspired commercial model of broadcasting has been globalised, creating a dynamic media, challenging state censorship and widening the public sphere, while at the same time also leading to the concentration of media power among private corporations (Thussu, 2015).

The exponential growth of multichannel networks has made the global media landscape multicultural, multilingual and multinational. Digital communication technologies in broadcasting and broadband have given viewers in many countries the ability to access simultaneously a vast array of local, national, regional, and international television in various genres. The last decade witnessed an exponential growth in the number of 24-hour news channels around the world (Rai and Cottle, 2010). Changing not only broadcasting ecology globally but affecting social and political sphere, real-time news has reinvented itself over the years and made a mark on the journalism industry. It has grown to influence the political decision-making and empower the social movements across the world (Cushion and Lewis, 2010).

The media, especially broadcasting, retains an important position as an instrument of global influence and, ever since the Cold War, international broadcasting has been a part of foreign policy agenda. Until the globalisation of television and telecommunication, international broadcasters fulfilled an important information gap, especially in countries where media were under strict state control. With the deregulation and digitisation of communication and the entry of powerful private providers, the broadcasting landscape has been altered, offering new challenges and opportunities. There are various types of new media flows—some emanating from European nations, based on old colonial patterns—notably Britain's BBC World News and France 24—as well as more recent content emerging from the global South (Thussu, 2007a). Russia has raised its international

growing competition for audiences and, crucially, advertising revenue, has intensified. Not dissimilar to trends in the US, the growing commercialisation of television news has forced broadcast journalists and television producers in India to recognise the need to make news entertaining. They borrow and adapt ideas from entertainment and adopt an informal style with an emphasis on personalities, storytelling and spectacle (Thussu, 2007b; Bhusan, 2013).

As cross-media ownership rules are relaxed, there is greater inclination towards concentration of media power: non-media groups have invested heavily in television and telecommunication. Increasingly large companies are establishing across various segments of the media and entertainment world: new 'media conglomerates', drawing their inspiration from the US model, are in the making. One prominent example is Reliance, one of India's largest conglomerates, which since 2013 owns Network 18, the company that also operates CNN/IBN, one of India's leading English language news networks. As in the US, where such moves have been reinforced by the takeover of news networks by huge media corporations, and whose primary interest is in the entertainment business: notable examples include Viacom-Paramount (CBS News), Disney (ABC News), Time-Warner (CNN), and News Corporation (Fox News), in India too, media conglomerates who make profit in entertainment industry have investments in news networks. Such ownership structures can be reflected in the type of stories—about celebrities from the world of entertainment and sport, for example—that receive prominence on news, thus strengthening corporate synergies.

In the process, symbiotic relationships between the news and new forms of current affairs and factual entertainment genres, such as reality TV have developed, blurring the boundaries between news, documentary and entertainment. Such hybrid programming feeds into and benefits from the 24x7 news cycle: providing a feast of visually arresting, emotionally-charged infotainment that sustains ratings and keeps production costs low. The growing global popularity of such infotainment-driven programming indicates the success of this formula (Thussu, 2007b). In India, as one commentator has noted, entertainment and infotainment dominate the "ABC of

Media—Advertising, Bollywood and Corporate Power" (Sainath, 2010).

Television News as 'Bollywoodised' Infotainment

In a fiercely competitive and crowded market such as the one in India, news networks are under constant pressure to raise their ratings and acquire new programming to ensure regular stream of advertising revenue. There is a tendency to make news entertaining, which in the context of India means drawing on Bollywood or Bollywoodised content. Such infotainment fare is now common practice on news networks which regularly broadcast 'exclusive' stories about the supernatural and the bizarre as examples of compelling TV. There is a noticeable change in style and content away from a considered, professional approach to a flashier and visually more dynamic presentation; the emphasis seems to be not on the journalistic skills of news anchors and reporters but on how they look on camera, with style taking precedence over substance. An informal, entertaining schedule is created to increase the audience base across the channels, ratings and revenues delivering programmes—sports, entertainment and lifestyle—have increased, while news and analysis have shown a corresponding decline.

Is commodification of television news and its growing politicisation expanding or eroding the public discourse in the world's largest democracy? Given the symbolic and semiotic power of television news, is infotainment-driven television news contributing towards making India a producer and consumer of commodity capitalism?

Given the obsession with Bollywoodised content and its regionalised clones that characterise much of television content, the 'public' aspects of news seem to have been undermined (Rajagopal, 2009). The popularisation of celebrity-driven and sensationalist news may have made it a more marketable commodity, but this has also debased public discourse, increasingly aiming at the lowest common denominator. With a few honourable exceptions, much of television news has almost negligible reporting of rural poverty or the regular suicides of small farmers or of developmental issues in general, as they rarely translate into ratings or interest advertisers, on whose support the edifice of commercial television news is ultimately based. It has been suggested that in a market-driven economy, the media system "is not only closely linked to the *ideological* dictates of the business-run society, it is also an integral element of the economy" (McChesney, 1999: 281, italics in original).

If excessive marketisation has contributed to privileging sport and celebrity spectacle in the news, the shift from bureaucrats to marketing executives has also influenced the politics of television news. News is increasingly shrill, bipartisan and noisy. During Doordarshan's monopoly of broadcast news, news on television was considered little more than the government's view of the day's events, with only primary definers of news—mostly politicians and other elite groups—dominating the discourse. In terms of presentation and style, the news was bland and bureaucratic: audience interest did not matter, as there was no competition with private television. This interest in news may reflect not only the low baseline from which it started, but also the popularity and diversity of debate in a complex political scene and the 'argumentative' nature of Indians (Sen, 2005). News in Hindi and in other major languages in India has a much wider audience base than the elite English language networks (Ninan, 2007).

As most of television news is in private control, what happens to the public aspects of broadcasting in a country where, despite strong economic growth, more than 400 million people live in poverty—the world's largest chunk of poor people in a single country? The infotainment-driven television news has not yet reached large parts of rural and semi-urban India, where Doordarshan still reigns supreme, despite severe competition from private news networks—especially in cable and satellite homes. In 2013, Doordarshan was reaching more than 500 million viewers, while DD News, the first and the only terrestrial news channel in the country, had the highest reach into television households. Although not as bland as during its monopoly days, DD News still lacks the edge and critical dimension that at least some private channels have earned in the past decade of operation. As Cottle and Rai (2008: 77) suggest, "In a diverse and plural polity such as India, the communicative structures of television news are particularly important in that they variously enable or disable the public elaboration of conflicting interests and identities." Networks such as NDTV 24x7 have arguably broadened the public discourse in India, bringing on board, for example, questions about environmental protection and right to information. The network has undertaken campaigns to promote particular causes and generated both revenues and more importantly awareness on issues such as protecting India's national animal, the tiger. Such instances may be characterised by what Cottle and Rai (2008: 83) have called "the campaigning frame", which "declares the news outlet's stance on a particular issue or cause and typically seeks to galvanise sympathies and support for its intervention, political or otherwise, beyond the world of journalism."

Diasporic Dimension

Since the 1990s, a new kind of migration from India—a middle-class migration—has brought with it Indian media to the rest of the world. The opening up of the media sphere in India, part of India's gradual integration in global neo-liberal capitalism, has in return given a boost to Indians abroad. Digitisation and the growing availability of satellite and cable television as well as online delivery mechanisms, have ensured that Indian media content—films, sports, entertainment and news—are regularly consumed among the diaspora. Indian television has been active in selling the global Indian to Indian audiences, and glitz and glamour of Bollywood to the famed NRIs (non-resident Indians). The 25-million strong Indian diaspora, scattered around the globe, have excelled in many spheres of life and enriched the cultural, economic and intellectual experience of countries like the US and Britain. They have also made a significant contribution to India's emergence as an economic and cultural power. The net worth of the Indian diaspora is estimated to be $300 billion and their annual contribution to the Indian economy valued at up to $10 billion (Kapur, 2010; Amrith, 2011; Thussu, 2013). As more professional migration becomes a reality, English language news channels and news portals provide information and analysis to keep abreast of developments in the home country.

In a globalised and interconnected world, depending on their economic and political influence within the centres of global power, diasporas can be a vital strategic instrument and channel of communication to further foreign policy goals and gains. Varadarajan has argued that diasporic relationships reflect globalised neo-liberal economics as well as the changing notions of territoriality. She conceptualises this as what she called the "domestic abroad," suggesting that "the production of the domestic abroad rests on the constitution of diasporas as subjects of an expanded, territorially diffused nation" (Varadarajan, 2010: 6). This diffused community has emerged in recent years as a vocal and valuable voice in the global arena. Its most articulate and effective manifestation is the growing presence of members of the Indian diaspora in Ivy League universities, international media and multilateral organisations, as well as in transnational corporations.

Communicating Indian presence among the leading US-based journalistic outlets has been facilitated by the fact that many Indians have reached the apex position in top-ranking US media: prominent examples include: Bobby Ghosh, Editor of *Time International*; Fareed Zakaria, Editor-at-large of *Time* and a leading CNN Commentator; Tunku Varadarajan has had various senior positions as Editor of *Newsweek International*; Raju Nerisetti headed digital operations at *Wall Street Journal* and was formerly Managing Editor of *The Washington Post*, while another Indian, Rajiv Chandrasekaran, was the National Editor of the same newspaper; Nikhil Deogun was Managing Editor at CNBC; while *Huffington Post* had Jimmy Soni as its Managing Editor. In London too, within the mainstream British media, Krishnan Guru-murthy at Channel 4 News, Nisha Pillai of the BBC World News and the *Guardian* columnist Aditya Chakraborty are examples of Indian presence; in 2013, Amol Rajan became the first Indian-origin Editor of a British national newspaper, *The Independent* (Thussu, 2013). As Tharoor has noted, the diaspora's active presence on the social media debating and discussing India-related issues wields "a disproportionate influence on international perceptions of India" (Tharoor, 2012: 307).

Another major constituency for Indian news is the Indian corporates: more than 700 Indian companies were operating in Britain in 2012, with such blue-chip corporations such as Tata—which owns luxury brands British Jaguar and Land Rover—becoming the biggest private sector employer in the country. A new market of news is the growing presence of Indian students in universities in the US and UK—India is the second largest source of overseas students in the US-UK higher education sector after China.

The instantaneous and 24x7 availability of news from India provides the Indian diaspora with access to the latest national information. The growth of online content emanating from India, particularly relevant for the younger generation of these communities, is reformulating the sense of India among this demographic which, as Kapur (2010: 15) suggests, "...given India's demographics and those of industrialised countries, international migration from India will continue to grow, as will the diaspora's reshaping of both India and its destination countries."

Indian TV News in the Global Media Sphere

The growing profile of India on the global scene has been helped by the increasing visibility of its cultural and creative industries, its diaspora, and its media operating in a vibrant and expanding media sphere in one of the world's fastest growing economies (despite the global economic downturn, in 2013, India still posted an economic growth of 5%). Given the size and scale of the Indian television industry and the globalisation of Indian businesses, the Indian version of news has potentially an audience base, beyond the diasporic one.

Unlike those in the Western world, the media and cultural industries in India are growing rapidly: in 2012, the Indian entertainment and media industry was worth $29 billion, with a steady annual growth rate. International investment is increasing in India's media sector, as cross-media ownership rules are relaxed (Kohli-Khandekar, 2013; FICCI/KPMG Report, 2013). At the same time, Indian media companies are also investing outside national territories. In the past two decades, India has become an important

about India. Uniquely Indian themes such as yoga, Ayurveda or Bollywood are obvious areas but information about Indian business successes and the richness and diversity of the country need prominence.

According to India's Ministry of External Affairs estimates, DD News was reaching just 36 overseas markets—down from over 100. Where it was available, the audience was extremely small and, as a free-to-air channel, it received very meagre advertising revenue. There have been suggestions to seek reciprocal landing rights in different markets so, for example, if France 24 is available in India, DD News should be given access in France. Another suggestion is to have direct deals with leading international hotel chains, where executives and elites consume international news. One other possibility is to use Antrix, the commercial arm of the government-run Indian Space Research Organisation (ISRO), to negotiate with satellite providers for whom they are important customers and seek access to global markets on a reciprocal basis. It may also use existing distribution networks that work with private Indian operators such as NDTV or even global networks like Star, to explore platform-sharing (Prasar Bharati, 2014).

Indian News Online?

One potential area for growth is online news. The global presence of Indian news media is likely to expand with the convergence of communications technologies and content *via* the Internet. As an industry report on India notes: "the number of internet users is expected to cross 546 million users by 2016, increasingly driven by wireless connections" (FICCI/KPMG Report, 2013). The most explosive growth is in mobile communication, as India is already one of the planet's biggest mobile phone markets. However, internet penetration remains very low: as of 2013, nearly 200 million Indians had internet access, a penetration rate of just over 18 per cent of India's 1.2 billion population. There is no doubt that with the growth of mobile internet, making 3G phones affordable and accessible, the penetration rate will accelerate. As elsewhere, young people in India are the biggest consumers, as well as producers of mobile digital content and of social media (such social media sites as Facebook are extremely popular among young Indians) (FICCI-KPMG Report, 2013).

What makes Indian case particularly noteworthy is the scale and scope of the potential change: India, even though an ancient civilisation, is a very young nation with more than 65 per cent of Indians being below the age of 35. As more members of this demographics join the online world, it is interesting to speculate what kind of content will be circulating on the electronic superhighways when not 18 but 90 per cent of Indians are able to use the Internet. As their connectivity grows, a sizeable segment of young Indians will increasingly be going online, producing, distributing and consuming media. Given their proficiency in English, the dominant language of global commerce and communication, coupled with the growth of English-language media in India and the globalisation of Indian media industries, they are likely to be more visible in international media sphere. The expert committee has suggesting setting up Prasar Bharati Connect (PBC), which would be tasked with managing DD website "to make them more appealing, interactive, and engaging, and also integrate them with the existing social media channels" (Prasar Bharati, 2014: 33).

A Voice of the Global South?

As one of the founder members of the Non-Aligned Movement, India pursued a largely autonomous foreign policy. It was a leading voice during the 1970s and 1980s debates within UNESCO about the creation of a New World Information and Communication Order. India was a founder member of the Non-aligned News Agencies Pool, an attempt to encourage South-South news exchange to counter Western information hegemony. As new international affiliations such as BRICS (which groups Brazil, Russia, India, China and South Africa) take shape—coinciding with cracks within the neo-liberal model of US-led capitalism—India could play a bigger role as a voice of the global South in international forums (Nordenstreng and Thussu, 2015).

Will the presence of Indian news on the international scene pose challenges to the Western-dominated news agendas? One key area where a global Indian news presence could make a meaningful difference is in the field of development news. India remains home to the world's largest population of poor people: on every major indices of social progress, it shows abysmally low ranking, despite demonstrating robust economic growth and lifting millions out of poverty in the past two decades. India and Indian media therefore have a moral and material imperative to be at the forefront of shaping discourse about how to deploy media and communication tools for poverty alleviation programmes internationally. They can draw on a rich legacy and a long-standing tradition of Mahatma Gandhi's egalitarian journalism (the iconic leader of India's independence movement edited for most of his political life the weekly newspaper *Young India*, later renamed *Harijan*).

More broadly, Indian journalism evolved within the context of a fight for democracy in the tradition of anti-colonialism, represented by leaders like Gandhi. After independence, a 'Third Worldist,' anti-imperialist ideology—sometimes more as a rhetoric than reality—continued to define mainstream media under Nehruvian socialism. Making use of this legacy of elegantly articulating the voice of the global South, it can make real contribution to international debates, beyond World Bank-dictated anti-poverty programmes. As digital media and communication become more commercialised, India's could be an important voice in articulating Southern viewpoints and perspectives in global forums like UNESCO, International Telecommunication Union (ITU) and World Intellectual Property Organisation (WIPO) on diverse and contested issues such as multiculturalism, intellectual property rights in the digital environment, safeguarding of media plurality and indigenous media.

Would an Indian media perspective on events in other developing countries be less affected by the colonial mindset? The proliferation of news networks and the multiplicity of other media outlets have contributed to the freedom from government control and arguably democratised public communication. In such a news environment, citizens have access to a wider range of information and journalists can help to give voice to disadvantaged and seek accountability from politicians and bureaucrats (Roy, 2012). From electoral politics to economy, to development issues, television news has a major role in shaping public opinion. Networks like NDTV 24x7 have taken up causes in the public interest—such as rural development, environmental protection, freedom of information, and gender equality. Their efforts have at times influenced government policy. There is also a strong and growing tradition of investigative journalism to expose social and political misdemeanours, corruption and criminality.

However, such public-interest journalism is confined to a few notable exceptions. Most of television news is entrenched in a Bollywoodised media culture, thriving on entertainment and infotainment-driven programming rooted in a crassly commercial media system. By overwhelming public discourse with Bollywoodised content, egalitarian aspects are marginalised in the news media, at a time when more than 400 million people in India remain illiterate and the gap between the rich and the poor is growing, thereby making India one of the world's most unequal societies, despite a vigorous democratic political system and impressive economic growth.

The issues that confront the Indian situation—about governance, sustainable development, pervasive poverty—have striking resonances in many other countries in the global South. Despite India's gradual integration with the US-led neo-liberal economic system, as a producer and a consumer of commodity capitalism, there is a strong and deeply-entrenched tradition of argumentation and critical conversation in the Indian body politic and in its intellectual life, reflected also in journalistic discourses (Sen, 2005; Rajagopal, 2009). As Indian media globalise, will this critical mass contribute to strengthening the voice of the global South; of those at the receiving end of the excesses of neo-liberalism, or will India play second fiddle to the US media, acting as surrogate supplement to the US-dominated entertainment-driven news?

References

Amrith, Sunil (2011). *Migration and Diaspora in Modern Asia*. Cambridge: Cambridge University Press.

Athique, Adrian (2012). *Indian Media*. Cambridge: Polity.

Bhusan, Bharat (2013). "News in Monochrome: Journalism in India", *Index on Censorship* 42(36): 37-42.

Chaudhuri, Maitrayee (2010). "Indian Media and its Transformed Public", *Contributions to Indian Sociology* 44(1-2): 57-78.

Cottle, Simon and Mugdha Rai (2008). "Television News in India: Mediating Democracy and Difference", *International Communication Gazette* 70(1): 76-96.

Cushion, Stephen and Justin Lewis (eds.) (2010). *The Rise of 24-Hour News Television: Global Perspectives*. New York: Peter Lang.

FICCI-KPMG Report (2013). *The Power of a Billion: Realizing the Indian Dream. FICCI-KPMG Indian Media and Entertainment Industry Report 2013*. Mumbai: Federation of Indian Chambers of Commerce and Industry.

Hallin, Daniel and Paolo Mancini (2004). *Comparing Media Systems: Three Models of Media and Politics*. Cambridge: Cambridge University Press.

Kapur, Davesh (2010). *Diaspora, Development, and Democracy: The Domestic Impact of International Migration from India*. Princeton: Princeton University Press.

Kohli-Khandekar, Vanita (2013). *The Indian Media Business*. Fourth edition. New Delhi: Sage.

McChesney, Robert (1999). *Rich Media, Poor Democracy: Communication Politics in Dubious Times*. Champaign, IL.: University of Illinois Press.

Ninan, Sevanti (2007). *Headlines from the Heartland: Reinventing the Hindi Public Sphere*. New Delhi: Sage.

Nordenstreng, Kaarle and Daya Kishan Thussu (eds.) (2015). *Mapping BRICS Media*. London: Routledge.

Prasar Bharati (2014). *Report of the Expert Committee on PrasarBharati. Vol. I and II*. New Delhi, Government of India: Prasar Bharati.

Rajagopal, Arvind (ed.) (2009). *The Indian Public Sphere: Readings in Media History*. New York: Oxford University Press.

Roy, Srirupa (2011). "Television News and Democratic Change in India", *Media, Culture & Society* 33(5): 761-77.

Sainath, Palagummi (2010). "How to Feed Your Billionaires", *The Hindu*, 17 April.

Schaefer, David and Kavita Karan (eds.) (2013). *Bollywood and Globalisation: The Global Power of Popular Hindi Cinema*. London: Routledge.

Seib, Philip (2012). *Real-Time Diplomacy: Politics and Power in the Social Media Era*. New York: Palgrave Macmillan.

Sen, Amartya (2005). *The Argumentative Indian*. London: Penguin.

Tharoor, Shashi (2012). *PaxIndica: India and the World of the Twenty-First Century*. New Delhi: Penguin. p.56.

Thussu, Daya Kishan (2007a). "Mapping Global Media Flow and Contra-Flow", in Daya Kishan Thussu (ed.), *Media on the Move: Global Flow and Contra-Flow*. London: Routledge. pp.11-32.

———. (2007b). *News as Entertainment: The Rise of Global Infotainment*. London: Sage.

———. (2013). *Communicating India's Soft Power: Buddha to Bollywood*. New York: Palgrave/Macmillan.

———. (2015). *International Communication: Continuity and Change*. Third Edition. London: Bloomsbury Academic.

Zhu, Ying (2012). *Two Billion Eyes: The Story of China Central Television*. New York: The New Press.

Section II

Policy/Context

The News Broadcasters Association (NBA), formed in 2007, comprises leading broadcasters and was set up to represent their interests. The News Broadcasters Standards (Dispute Redressal) Authority (later called the News Broadcasters Standards Authority [NBSA]), was launched on 2 October 2008, barely a month before the 26 November 2008 Mumbai terror attacks, which drew widespread criticism of television coverage of the attacks.

The Indian Broadcasting Federation (IBF) set up the Broadcasting Content Complaints Council (BCCC), a self-regulatory mechanism for General Entertainment Channels (GEC) or the non-news and current affairs channels, in June 2011. Retired judges of the Supreme Court head the NBSA and the BCCC.

Regulation, in whatever form it takes, is a contentious issue. All over the world, different models of regulation have been attempted with varying success. In a paper examining self-regulation and the media, Angela Campbell outlines five factors responsible for the success or failure of self-regulation. These are industry incentives, the ability of government to regulate, the use of measurable standards, public participation, and industry structure. Clearly, in India, while the first three exist in some form, the latter two are either non-existent or weak.

In successive annual reports, from the very first report in 2007-08 to the annual report for 2013-14, the NBA stressed the importance of self-regulation by a "jury of peers". Self-regulation, the outgoing NBA President K.V.L. Narayan Rao said, was a means for broadcasters to "avoid governmental interference."[1]

But self-regulation is more than a means to avoid governmental interference. It is perhaps the most demonstrable evidence that the media is aware of its responsibility and is willing to hold itself accountable to the scrutiny of its peers as well as of society. Effective self-regulation helps the media establish trust and credibility with its readers and audience.

---

1. Message from K.V.L. Narayan Rao, President, News Broadcasters Association, *Annual Report 2013-14*.

While the big media corporations view freedom from governmental interference as a free speech issue, there is no doubt that preserving and protecting freedom of expression is all the more crucial in a chaotic media environment, with state-controlled public broadcasting, private print and broadcast media and a non-corporate or non-governmental media that seeks to occupy a community media space.

Untrammelled Growth

The broadcast industry had grown exponentially in the post-liberalisation phase, with private television channels growing from 2 in 1992 to 792 by March 2014. If only 1 channel (Aaj Tak) was given permission in 2000, by the end of 2001, 39 television channels had begun uplinking from India,[2] with the number steadily rising to the present 792.

A FICCI-KPMG report[3] estimated the value of the country's media and entertainment (M&E) industry at ₹ 918 billon in 2013, as it registered a growth of 11.8 per cent over 2012. The report said that, by 2013, there were 161 million TV households, 94,067 newspapers (12,511 dailies), about 2,000 multiplexes and 214 million internet users of which 130 million are mobile internet users. In the next four years, the figure was expected to touch ₹ 1.78 trillion (US$ 28.95 billion).

But this growth was by no means a smooth and even one. There have been sneak mergers and acquisitions, channels had closed down and media owners arrested for alleged involvement in ponzi schemes (a fraudulent investing scam), as in the case of the Saradha chit fund scam, which also led to the collapse of 6 television channels, 8 newspapers and an FM radio station, besides rendering around 1,600 journalists jobless overnight.

Apart from these malpractices, ownership of broadcast media is predominantly in the hands of big business and politicians. The

2. See list compiled :*http://www.cablequest.org/pdfs/broadcaters/Permitted-Private-Channels-List-20-03-2013-status_220313.pdf*
3. The stage is set: FICCI-KPMG Indian Media and Entertainment Industry Report 2014.

growing corporatisation of the media in India and the lack of any restrictions on cross-media ownership has resulted in a very uneven playing field, where a few companies manage to control a larger share of the market. The real challenge, writes media commentator Paranjoy Guha Thakurta, is to "ensure that growing concentration of ownership in an oligopolistic market does not lead to loss of heterogeneity and plurality" (The Hoot, 2012).

While the business of broadcast media calls for much more scrutiny than it attracts at the moment, there has been much discussion and research into the content of television and its influence on society. In the two decades following liberalisation of the economy and the burgeoning media industry, general entertainment channels have proliferated, and along with them, a host of programming marked by soap operas, game shows, competitive music and dance and reality shows.

The early years of broadcast media in India brought much excitement about the potential of the medium. The advent of private television channels and the increase in news channels, heralded the promise of independent news that was freed of the stranglehold of the 'official' news purveyed by Doordarshan—India's state-funded and state-controlled public broadcaster.

But things began to pall as news channels began to broadcast 'breaking news' on a 24x7 basis, each screaming an 'exclusive' even as footage was the same or looped continuously. Competition and the race for TRPs and advertising, which was the primary source of revenue for general entertainment television, also began in the arena of news, substantially altering the nature of news coverage in broadcast media.

The CMS Media Lab study of the percentage of the total news time of different categories of news between 2005-2013 is indicative of the trends of coverage. The study covered prime-time (7-11 pm) coverage of six national news channels—Aaj Tak, CNN IBN, DD News, NDTV 24x7, Star News/ABP News and Zee News. National politics, the highest category of all, which started at 11.60 per cent in 2005, dropped inexplicably to 4.25 per cent in 2007 and then climbed steadily to 20.74 per cent. Sports, which is the other big category for media coverage, has fluctuated between 10.70 per cent in 2005 to 20.97 in 2008, dropping to 10.04 per cent in 2013. Film and entertainment was the third highest category of 2013 at 9.58 per cent of the total coverage.

Crime, which clocked 9.4 per cent in 2005 and went up to 11.06 per cent in 2007, dropped to 4.61 per cent the next year and climbed again to 5.74 per cent by 2011 to reach 8.31 per cent in 2013. All other categories, from accidents, art, civic issues, education, science and technology, human interest stories, etc., barely got much play in prime time news. Agriculture, which fluctuated between 0.10 in 2005 to 0.29 percent in 2008, actually began falling steadily in 2011 (0.09), 2012 (0.08) and 2013 (0.05), despite the number of deaths of farmers throughout these years.

The channel-wise news content trends reveal the inherent focus and priority of each channel. Star News, Zee News and Aaj Tak, for instance, consistently emphasised national politics, sports, crime and film and entertainment with percentages of coverage going into double digits. In 2013 alone, the percentage or coverage of national politics, for instance, was 21.69 per cent (Aaj Tak) and 16.91 per cent (Zee News).

In 2005, *Outlook* magazine devoted a special issue to the "dumbing down" of news—from inaccuracies and bad reporting, the "sexing it up... sting operations with methods and morals mixed up, breaking news a dozen times a day on TV and selling of editorial space".

Writing on the impact of Star News in India, Daya Kishan Thussu (2007) bemoaned the emphasis on the four 'C' formula in India (an Indian adaptation from the three 'S' formula of Rupert Murdoch's media: sex, sensationalism and sport). Indeed, the debacle over illegal privacy intrusions in Murdoch's News of the World in the United Kingdom (UK) had led to the Leveson enquiry[4] and the setting up of a Press Complaints Commission in the UK.

As Ed Richards, Chief Executive of the British communications regulator Ofcom, puts it, "freedom of expression is at the heart of

---

4. Leveson Inquiry: Culture, Practice and Ethics of the Press, *http://webarchive.nationalarchives.gov.uk/20140122145147/http://www.levesoninquiry.org.uk/about/the-report/*

regulation."[5] And, given the revelations of intrusive practices of the News of the World, this would imply protecting people from privacy violations as well as harmful and illegal content, besides ensuring plurality and diversity in the media.

Intrusive Broadcast Media

India has also had a host of similar privacy intrusions by broadcast news media—from Zee Television's arrogant adoption of a socio-judicial role in its hosting and airing of a 'live' *panchayat* in 2004 to decide the fate of a hapless 'Gudiya' to the shocking intrusion of a television crew into the home of an Aligarh Muslim University (AMU) Prof Shrinivas Ramchandra Siras in February 2010, disrupting what was clearly a private and consensual sexual interaction between the professor and an adult man. The circulation of the video led to the suspension of the professor, which was later revoked following a court order, but the professor committed suicide in April 2010.

In an open letter[6] to the media, women's organisations and women's rights activists expressed their anger at media intrusions. "We are appalled by at the media's (especially television) coverage of the 'Gudiya-Taufiq-Arif' case. We strongly resent the growing instances of trial by media, the media's self-appointed role as resolvers of conflict, and the use of people's personal tragedies to increase network ratings. Headlines like 'Kiski Gudiya?' also symbolised the regressive image of women as property that informed the media's coverage." Rather than resolving conflict, as Zee and others claimed to be doing, the media enhanced conflict in this case by forcing relatives to give public statements against one another, the letter added.

In the Siras case, an independent fact-finding committee of civil rights activists and lawyers sought action against the television journalists Syed Adil Murtaza of TV 100 and Ashu Misam of Voice of Nation "for trespassing, violating privacy and intimidation of Dr Siras

5. Broadcasting regulation in a converged world, 16 October 2013. Speech for the Centre for Law Justice & Journalism annual lecture.

6. Extract from 'Open Letter to the Media', 30 September 2004, available at *sacw.net*.

at his home." They also demanded an investigation by police as to whether the journalists were acting independently or on behalf of the AMU authorities. The two journalists were arrested but there is little information about action taken against their television channels.[7]

In 2004, there was no self-regulation in broadcast news media. No formal complaint was lodged against Zee News in the Gudiya case. By 2010, self-regulation of broadcast news media was two years old, but the television channels involved in the Siras case were still beyond its purview and action, such as it were, could only be taken by the criminal justice system.

Demand for Regulation

For more than a decade, there were demands from civil society and even the government for an independent regulator and even for a statutory regulator for broadcast media. But the nature of this regulation, whether statutory or independent and self-regulated, was always a contested issue.

Early on, senior editors and news presenters were conscious of the perils of competition and of the medium's limitations. In 2006, the respected magazine Seminar, devoted a special issue to the media. The views of those in the centre of the growth of private news channels make for interesting reading. The television anchor and then Editor-in chief of IBN 18 Network, Rajdeep Sardesai (2006) said that television was emerging from "a period when it was little more than a first information report to a medium which can, if you try hard enough, actually set the agenda." He admitted that there was a serious crisis of content on television and the competition had led to the growing 'tabloidisation' of the medium.

In the same issue, television anchor and news presenter Karan Thapar (2006), says that television news had an inherent tendency to sensationalise, apart from having two limitations, both of which are hardly ever acknowledged. The first is that television has problems with news it cannot show and thus ignores news that cannot be filmed.

7. Avanti Media Limited owns TV 100, broadcasting from 2006, and Northern India Holdings Pvt Ltd owns Voice of Nation, broadcasting in digital mode from 2010. *Source*: List of permitted private satellite TV channels as on 20 March 2013, *www.cablequest.org*.

television channels and monitors about 210 channels on a 24x7 basis today. Set up in 2008, it monitors content of all television channels for violation of programme codes and private FM radio channels. The television channels are chosen at random from the 839 channels currently beaming into Indian homes. The government hopes to increase the capacity of the EMMC to cover 1500 channels by 2017.[10]

The NBA has taken on the mantle of self regulation for news channels through the NBSA, while the IBF, formed in 1999 to represent the fledgling broadcasting industry, set up the BCCC in 2011 to monitor and address complaints against all non-news and current affairs TV channels or the General Entertainment Channels (GECs).[11]

There are other regulatory authorities, including a statutory one for film—the Central Board of Film Certification (CBFC) addresses content relating to films, film trailers or movie videos, and a non-statutory, self-regulatory body for advertising—the Advertising Standards Council of India (ASCI).

The NBA and its regulatory body, the NBSA, has been lobbying with the government for making its code a statutory one. This was granted to advertising agencies in August 2006. The ASCI addresses advertisement-related complaints and the self-regulatory body for advertising agencies lobbied successfully to accord its code a statutory status.[12] In August 2006, the Cable Television Network Rules, 1994, were amended and Rule 7 (9) reads: "No advertisement which violates the Code for self regulation in advertising, as adopted by the Advertising Standards Council of India, Mumbai, for public exhibition in India from time to time, shall be carried in the cable service".

Despite their own codes, both news and non-news channels are governed by the programme code as spelt out in Rule 6 of the Cable

10. Statement of Minister of State for Information and Broadcasting, Rajyavardhan Singh Rathore in Parliament, reported in Indiantelevision.com, *http://www.indiantelevision.com/regulators/i-and-b-ministry/electronic-media-monitoring-centre-to-go-up-to-1500-channels-by-2017-rathore-141210*

11. See IBF website: *http://www.ibfindia.com/history-vision*

12. *http://www.ascionline.org/images/pdf/asci_code2new.pdf*

Television Networks Rules, 1994. This is a singularly myopic piece of work, spelling out a range of programming that is prohibited on grounds of obscenity, good taste or decency. The code for instance, prohibits any programme that 'contains visuals or words which reflect a slandering, ironical and snobbish attitude in the portrayal of certain ethnic, linguistic and regional groups'.

The NBA's code has a number of do's and don't's in the reporting of crime, depiction of violence against women and children, of sex and nudity (qualifying this guideline to say the intent is 'not to be moralistic or prudish, and this self-regulation is aimed not at moral policing, but rather at ensuring that overtly regressive and explicit acts and visuals do not slip into broadcasts'), privacy, sting operations and the broadcast of 'material that glorifies superstition and occultism in any manner'.

Although it does outline the responsibilities of broadcast media to 'adhere to the highest possible standards of public service and integrity', the code itself is silent about issues like paid news. In 2011, after discussions and directives from the Election Commission of India, the NBA came up with an advisory on paid news.[13]

But the 47th report of the Parliamentary Standing Committee related to IT (information technology), which was on "Issues Related to Paid News", observed that the existing regulatory set-up dealing with paid news was inadequate and an 'eye wash'.[14] The punitive powers of statutory regulators like the Press Council of India (PCI) and the EMMC were inadequate.

Highlighting the conflict of interest inherent in the appointment of media owners as members of the PCI or self-regulatory bodies, the committee recommended the establishment of either a single

13. "Norms & Guidelines on Paid News" dated 24 November 2011 issued by NBSA, states: 'Every news broadcasting organization shall disclose conspicuously in an appropriate manner during broadcast of a program, on their television channel/s and on their website/s, including during a news, current affairs, sports, entertainment or promotional broadcast as to whether the content of such broadcast has been paid for by or on behalf of the Entity that is subject matter of such broadcast in any manner whatsoever; and whether such broadcast is an "advertorial" or other media marketing initiative'.

14. The 47th report of the Parliamentary Standing Committee on Information Technology submitted to the Lok Sabha on 6 May 2013.

regulatory body for both print and electronic media or enhancing the punitive powers of the PCI and setting up a similar statutory body for electronic media. The committee said: "Such regulator(s) should have the power to take strong action against offenders and should not include media owners/interested parties as members".

The BCCC has dealt with a series of complaints but its track record has been abysmal. Supreme Court advocate Apar Gupta, in an analysis of its functioning, writes that the BCCC, which began as 'an alternative to rigid governmental regulation', was actually in danger of emulating the state (Gupta, 2013). Interestingly, Gupta adds, the BCCC, which was formed on 1 June 2011, received 'recognition' from the Delhi High Court barely two months later in the form of a judgement on the reality show *Sach ka Saamna*. An IMC had maintained that the programme was not 'adhering to good taste and decency' and issued a show cause notice to the channel, which, in turn, said that 'bureaucrats' were not the best people to monitor television content, a point accepted by the court.[15]

The court, while going into the question of regulation and acknowledging the self-regualtory mechanism of the BCCC, said that it was "important for the IMC to have a broad-based membership reflective of the competing interests involved in protecting the freedom of speech and expression guaranteed by the Constitution".

However, only a fraction of the over 700 television channels in India are members of the industry associations and the self-regulatory bodies they have set up. Several media houses have stayed away, remaining out of the purview of the industry-led self-regulatory mechanism. Some media houses, like Associated Broadcasting Company Pvt. Ltd., owners of the controversial TV9, which was an associate member of the NBA until 2011, dropped out later for reasons unstated.

In a panel discussion[16] on the media law consultation organised by the Law Commission in 2014, NBSA chairperson Justice Ravindran asked: "How can a voluntary body be effective when only

15. W. P. (C) 879/2010, Star India Private Limited *versus* Union of India, 30 September 2011.

16. *http://www.medianama.com/2014/10/223-media-regulation-india-self-regulation/*

60 are members? The 50-60 channels who are members of NBSA are ready to follow the rules. It is the others who refuse to come in, or have gone out. The regulations are meant for them".

Indeed, what happens to all the news channels—a whopping 333 channels—which don't come under the purview of the NBA? Which regulatory authority do they fall under?

Shaky Beginnings

Unlike the ASCI and the BCCC, the path to self-regulation for television news channels in India has not been smooth. Presently, it appears to have come full circle when it elected Rajat Sharma (LiveMint, 2014), chairman and editor-in-chief of India TV as the President of the NBA in 2014, five years after he walked out of the organisation as he was aggrieved at the decision of the News Broadcasting Standards (Disputes Redressal) Authority[17] to fine India TV for erroneous reportage.[18]

For the NBA, the beginnings of self-regulation could not have been more disastrous. This was its very first order after the NBSA (as it later came to be known) became operational on 2 October 2008, and here was a leading broadcaster walking out. Where was the much vaunted "monitoring from a jury of peers" that the organisation's website[19] proudly proclaimed? Or the "confidence in the fairness, balance and credibility" that the NBA's first President and the TV Today executive director, G. Krishnan, referred to in the association's first annual general meeting on 30 September 2008?

In its press release of 22 August 2008 to announce the constitution of the NBSA, the NBA said:

> ...the basic strength of a news channel lies in its credibility, from which flows its ability to influence public opinion. A censure emanating from a jury of its peers would indisputably affect the credibility of a channel. Besides, such a process is not without its legal ramifications. A channel acting in breach of established guidelines

17. Changed to News Broadcasting Standards Authority (NBSA) in 2009
18. See *http://www.exchange4media.com/35313_india-tv-returns-to-nba-fold-rajat-sharma-to-join-nba-board.html* and Rediff.com (2009).
19. News Broadcasters Association, *http://www.nbanewdelhi.com/about-nba.asp*

> could hardly defend its motives or suggest that it was acting fairly, if it is censured by a jury comprising its peers.
>
> Interference by government, however well intentioned, would however imperil not just independent journalism, but the very process of investigation itself. It therefore has become imperative that news channels lay down guidelines, procedural safeguards and establish a body that would act as a watchdog and a grievance redressal forum.
>
> The NBA had committed to the government, that as a measure of self-regulation it would put in place a Code of Ethics & Broadcasting Standards to be followed by its Members; and a News Broadcasting Standards Disputes Redressal Authority ("Authority") for enforcement of the Code.

Clearly, it was not going to be an easy task. In the wake of the criticism over the television coverage of the 26 November 2008 terror attacks on Mumbai, the clamour for stiffer and more effective regulation, if broadcasters failed to report news responsibly, was impossible to ignore.

The complaint against India TV was that it had dubbed an interview given by US-based writer and policy analyst Farhana Ali to Reuters news agency in Hindi and aired it, giving the impression the interview was conducted by India TV. The NBSA, in its order, had imposed a fine of ₹ 1 lakh. But India TV was aggrieved at the manner in which the order was passed, alleging that there was no quorum or its reply that it had issued an apology to the complainant was not taken cognisance of.

In this instance, India TV was persuaded to return three months later and given a place on the board of the association and its head, Rajat Sharma, even served as Treasurer in 2013-14, becoming its President the following year.

NBSA Complaints

Self-regulation of private broadcast news media in India is in its infancy. But in the five years since coming into operation, how has the NBSA acquitted itself?

The NBSA comprised a chairperson who was an eminent jurist and eight members, four of whom were eminent editors employed with a broadcaster and four others who had 'special knowledge and/or practical experience in the field of law, education, medicine, science, literature, public administration, consumer affairs, environment, human psychology and/or culture'.

All of them were nominated by the NBA board by a majority decision and receive an honorarium from the NBA.[20] A two-tier system was laid down where complainants could approach the broadcaster first and then complain to the NBSA if not satisfied. The NBSA had the power to warn, admonish, censure, express disapproval against and/or impose a fine upon the broadcaster and/or recommend to the concerned authority for suspension/revocation of license of such broadcaster. The fine amount was fixed at a maximum of ₹ 1 lakh.

The first chair of the NBSA was Justice J.S. Verma, former Chief Justice of India and former Chairperson of the National Human Rights Commission. Guiding the organisation as it took its fledgling steps until his demise in April 2013, Justice Verma laid the foundations for a self-regulatory process for news channels.

A complaints mechanism was set up and a 'Code of Ethics and Broadcasting Standards' was drawn up, spelling out the need for a 'jury of peers' to act as a watchdog and grievance redressal forum.[21] Besides, the NBA also formulated a number of guidelines and issued advisories from time to time, including guidelines for telecast of news during emergency situations and specific guidelines for reportage, besides a host of advisories such as those for reportage during the Mumbai terror attacks and the Kasab trial.

Successive annual reports of the NBA have expressed satisfaction that the organisation managed to put a redressal mechanism in

20. According to annual reports of the NBA, both chairpersons, Justice Verma and Justice Raveendran, chose not to claim their honorariums. The amount for others on the panel was first fixed at ₹ 5000 and enhanced to ₹ 10,000, while editorial representatives of members are not paid any honorarium.

21. Background, 'Code of Ethics and Broadcasting Standards', NBSA, *http://www.nbanewdelhi.com/pdf/final/NBA_code-of-ethics_english.pdf*

> the reportage was erroneous and defamatory comments were made by referring to them as "drunk", "half naked" and "nude" and further obfuscated the facts by employing editing tactics such as blurring out portions of one of their member's dress to make it appear that they were dressed in an indecent manner.

The NBSA order[22] said that the footage violated norms and that the broadcast intruded into the privacy of the students; there was no objectivity, impartiality or neutrality in reporting the incident; there was no verification of facts; and that it caused unwarranted distress to the students.' It imposed a fine of ₹ 1 lakh on Sakshi TV and directed it to air an apology expressing regrets for the broadcast.

But how effective is such regulation? Did the action deter Sakshi TV from such reportage in the future? In any case, no action could be taken against the other channels in the NALSAR case as they didn't fall within the purview of the NBA.

The NBSA's other moment of crisis came up in 2012 in the Zee News and Jindal Steel and Power Ltd (JSPL) sting-counter sting operations when JSPL's chairman Naveen Jindal accused Zee News Editor Sudhir Chaudhary and Zee Business Editor Samir Ahluwalia of trying to extort ₹ 100 crore from him in exchange for advertisements for stopping reportage on coal block allocations to the company.

JSPL filed a complaint with the PCI, which, in turn, referred it to the NBSA. Chaudhary had to resign as Treasurer of the Broadcast Editors Association (BEA), a body formed in 2009 to represent journalists in the broadcast industry. The NBSA, in the meantime, considered the complaint but since JSPL had also filed an FIR charging extortion as well as a defamation suit against Zee News, decided the matter was sub judice and could not be entertained.

In a study on self-regulation in television for a media watch site, The Hoot, Indira Akoijam observes that the BCCC and the NBA did not take 'strong punitive actions' against the channels that violated their guidelines (The Hoot, 2012). Warnings and admonitions, not to repeat the programme or directives to run an apology as a scroll, was

22. Order No. 26, Jan 6, 2014 *http://www.nbanewdelhi.com/pdf/28_ORDER%20NO%2026%20 DT.%206.1.14.pdf*

not enough. Stricter punishments, such as fines, would reduce the number of notices and less frequent violations, she felt.

The study also pointed out that the BCCC had received 239 complaints against news content in 2011. These were handed over to the NBA. But the latter only dealt with nine complaints between 2009-2011. Presumably, these were complaints directly filed with the NBA, but there is no information whether or not the complaints received through the BCCC were addressed at all.

There is also a need for a review of complaint procedures and whether these are loaded in favour of the broadcasting channels. Hearings are located in Delhi and complainants need to travel at their own cost to attend hearings and organise for their own assistance during hearings.

The NBSA appears to have put some system in place to monitor compliance with its orders. Since 2012-13, its annual reports have begun maintaining information on the compliance of broadcasters with the NBSA's orders and directives. But it remains to be seen how effective its orders are.

Regulation Tussles

While the industry has got codes and guidelines in place, the biggest incentive for the industry to regulate itself has been the threat of regulation. Periodically, the issue of a statutory regulator for broadcast media comes up, amidst protest from the private broadcast media companies and affirmations from the government that it is in favour of self-regulation and believes in protecting freedom of expression.

For a long time, the PCI, which is a statutory, quasi-judicial body set up by an act of Parliament to regulate print media, had been demanding that television too, come under the purview of a statutory regulator. Successive chairpersons of the PCI mooted the idea that its scope must extend to electronic media too.

In 2002, then Chairperson K. Jayachandra Reddy suggested that a regulator be appointed for electronic media. In 2006, amidst fears that the Broadcasting Services Regulation Bill 2006 would curb media freedom, the PCI said that a Media Council be set up as an independent self-regulatory body. In 2008, under the chairmanship of Justice G.N. Ray, the PCI reiterated its proposal to convert the Press Council into a 'Media Monitoring Commission of India'.[23] In 2011, the then Chairperson of PCI, Justice Markandeya Katju, proposed that electronic media be brought under the purview of PCI and that the organisation be renamed the Media Council.

Regrettably, the PCI is seen as an ineffective body, without much teeth beyond that of a censure. Its orders on complaints are delivered and directives on reportage are issued periodically, and it conducts *suo moto* inquiries on different issues, but there is no visible impact of these directives, and print media hardly ever acknowledges its orders, leave alone publishes them in the periodicals, as was the practice before.

A separate examination, beyond the scope of this paper, would be required to determine the causes for failure of the PCI to regulate print media. Suffice it is to say that the response of the print media industry, vital for any such regulatory exercise to be effective, is lacking.

Meanwhile, the NBA, several of whose members are also part of the PCI in their capacity as owners of print media, strongly criticised this move to set up a Media Council. The NBA, referring to an interview given by then PCI chairman, Justice Katju that self-regulation under Justice Verma had failed, wrote a letter to then Prime Minister Manmohan Singh dated 2 November 2011, seeking his intervention to "request the Chairman, PCI, to engage himself constructively with print media matters, which is the mandate he has under the Press Council Act and not to exceed his remit and to exercise restraint on commenting upon areas which are outside his jurisdiction." The NBA said it was consciously trying to regulate and improve broadcasting standards and that no unilateral steps should be taken to regulate electronic media.

The NBA had been lobbying with the government to strengthen its self-regulation efforts. In 2011, the NBA suggested that the Cable

23. Press Council of India Annual Report (1 April 2007-31 March 2008), p.6. *http://presscouncil.nic.in/OldWebsite/AR_COMPENDIUM/Annual -Report-07-08.pdf*

Television Networks (Regulation) Act, 1995 be amended such that the NBA's Code of Ethics and Redressal Regulations and Guidelines are made a part of the Programme Code under the Cable Television Networks Rules, thus giving it a statutory status.

But apart from content related issues, there are other contentious matters. For instance, which kind of regulator—a self-regulating body, a media council or an independent regulator—would be best able to tackle issues of cross-media ownership or policy matters like foreign direct investment (FDI) in the media or advertisements?

Unlike the PCI, which was set up by an Act of Parliament, the parent organisation of the NBSA, the NBA, is a not-for-profit company registered under the Companies Act. Its main objectives are to 'promote, aid, help, encourage, develop, protect and secure the interests of the news broadcasters in the Indian television Industry'. Its mandate includes lobbying with the government on advertising—support from Directorate of Advertising of Visual Publicity (DAVP) advertisements or the cap on advertisements, on carriage fees to be paid to MSOs (multi system operators), on the TRAI recommendations on cross-media ownership and other regulations affecting broadcast media, etc.

Self-regulation is one aspect of its objectives, albeit a very important one. But if the current government decides to push through with what it calls a 'super regulator', this self-regulation may be endangered.

The Communications Convergence Bill, 2000, had formulated provisions for a super regulator in the form of a Communication Commission of India (CCI), but the Indian Broadcasting Foundation (IBF) has staunchly opposed any such regulating body. The then NDA government had mooted this bill but was unable to carry it through. The UPA government, which succeeded it, ignored the bill.

Now, with a bigger mandate than before, the newly-elected NDA government is pushing for a single regulator to replace the Telecom Regulatory Authority of India (TRAI) and the Telecom Disputes Settlement and Appellate Tribunal (TDSAT). TRAI chairperson

Rajesh Khullar was quoted in media reports as saying that a regulator for both content and carriage was not feasible.[24]

But as media critic Sevanti Ninan (2009) put it, "the 'best way to never actually get media regulation on the ground is to announce a new bright idea every month. India has a flourishing industry of regulatory intent at this point." While government agencies announce various consultation papers and make recommendations on regulating broadcast media, the broadcast media industry, she said, is convinced that "Regulatory authorities are destroying the industry by populism".

In response to a Law Commission consultation on media laws earlier in 2014, the NBA pointed out that electronic media is already regulated by the Cable Television Networks (Regulation) Act, 1995, the Cable Television Networks Rules, 1994 and Policy Guidelines for Uplinking & Downlinking of Television Channels from India (content aspects) and the Telecom Regulatory Authority of India Act 1997, besides judicial decisions and guidelines and norms of bodies like the NBSA. The panel discussion[25] on media law consultation organised by the Law Commission elicited some discussion on regulation. NBSA chairperson Justice Ravindran said he preferred an "independent regulator," but didn't elaborate.

In an examination of the regulatory environment for Brazilian media, United Nations Educational, Scientific and Cultural Organization (UNESCO) consultants Toby Mendel and Eve Salomon outline the principles for an independent regulator.[26] These include laws that govern the media and funding for the office of the regulator and importantly, the very appointment of a regulator:

> Best practice suggests that broadcasting regulators should ideally consist of individuals with no personal connections to political or industry interests, and be nominated and appointed through a

24. "NDA rehashes old convergence bill, plans super regulator for telecom, TV and Internet", 8 September 2014. *http://firstbiz.firstpost.com/corporate/nda-rehashes-old-convergence-bill-plans-super-regulator-telecom-tv-internet-98008.html*

25. *http://www.medianama.com/2014/10/223-media-regulation-india-self-regulation/*

26. The Regulatory Environment for Broadcasting: An International Best Practice Survey for Brazilian Stakeholders, UNESCO debate series, February 2011, ISSN 2176-3224.

process which is itself detached from both politics and broadcasting, although this ideal is difficult, perhaps impossible, to realise fully.

Conclusion

For citizens, the media has acquired an all-powerful and omnipresent avatar and is seen as a law unto itself. While self-regulation is an ideal worth striving for, the choice is limited to the existing self-regulation mechanism by the broadcast media industry and that imposed by the state. An examination of the efficacy of self-regulation in broadcast news media must include a scrutiny of the involvement of the public at large, and a debate on how the agency of the audience can be developed and nurtured to ensure more accountability of the media.

Regulatory mechanisms, both of the state as well as by corporate bodies, have poor or notional public involvement. The public, as audiences or readers, are largely non-player, seven in terms of the debate and discussions around the issue of regulation. There's little discussion on an independent regulator.

The plight of media professionals in the broadcast media also impacts health of the industry. Already battling insecurity of employment and job losses (LiveMint, 2013) and facing the brunt of a demanding 24x7 work schedule, they are the foot soldiers who are attacked and even killed (Bhattacharjee, 2013) while on duty, and there's hardly any recognition of the role that conscientious media professionals working in broadcast media, independent of broadcast media owners, can play to strengthen media ethics and best practices.

Media awareness and education is nowhere near as developed as it should be and a healthy critique of media practices and impact is woefully lacking. There is a need for more rigorous public scrutiny of the media, its inherent biases and its structural limitations.

There's little transparency over media ownership and how it affects the regulation of media malpractices. The impact of ownership of the media by those who have strong business or political interests over self-regulation needs to be studied more rigorously, not merely in times of crisis (Caravan, 2013), but as an on-going exercise in accountability.

the same year—1993. By 1999, the joint venture unravelled leaving both of them free to broadcast what they wanted to. Foreign players were prohibited from news business.

But it was not until 2003, that the Murdoch-owned Star got into a joint news television venture with the Ananda Bazaar Patrika (ABP) Group called the Media Content and Communication Services India Limited (MCCS). For eight years, they operated together before calling it off.

The editorial control over news was with the MCCS, and Star had absolutely no control over the operations as Indian government rules confined foreign players to 26 per cent foreign direct investment (FDI) in news ventures. While Star was unhappy over the lack of control, ABP was unhappy about Star's joint venture with NDTV—an alliance restricted to sales. But for a little detour here.

For quite some time in the history of Indian news on television, one had to go to the hourly slots on public service broadcaster Doordarshan. Such was the wariness for allowing news in private hands, that it was not until the early 1990s that private players made their appearance on Doordarshan to broadcast news.

The first serious attempt to broadcast news by a private company was made in 1994 when production house NDTV was allowed to not to only air news, but also advertise it. The World This Week—as the name suggested—was a weekly round-up of events around the world on the newly launched Metro channel of Doordarshan. The arrangement continued for five years.

The 20-minute news capsule became an instant hit as it was different from the fare dished out by Doordarshan. As opposed to reading out the news, which was the format, events were being reported and analysed. The World This Week led to another production house, Living Media to come out with its news programme Aaj Tak—in Hindi. Doordarshan gave the satellite uplinking facilities to NDTV to produce the news. The production house was being paid ₹50,000 per episode. It was this 20-minute programme that made household names of Prannoy Roy, Appan Menon, and Rajdeep Sardesai. The World This Week had its share of controversies too. As this was a sponsored programme on a government platform, every telecast was subject to audit. It was found that Doordarshan had paid NDTV more than what was due to them. In fact, as far as the arrangement between NDTV and DD is concerned, an audit found it had incurred DD a loss of ₹3.52 crores. An enquiry also revealed that DD had given producers of NDTV access—free of cost—to news footage from DD archives.[1]

Despite all the controversies, for the first time, an environment for production and consumption of news was created. A little before that, video news magazine Newstrack, was distributed for payment. But it was not until 1994 that viewers woke up to news from a private source. Viewers knew what The World This Week was all about or who its producers were.

It was also around this time that a regulatory mechanism was conceived. Perhaps in anticipation of a change in the news landscape. The Broadcast Bill of 1996-97 tried to put in place a mechanism and envisaged checks and balances on the dissemination of news. Most important, it tried to address the issue of cross-media, in the context of market monopolies. That is, an attempt was made to ensure that both horizontal and vertical integration of the media came with checks and balances. Anticipating private players, the Bill had envisaged monopolistic situations and therefore restrictions ostensibly served the purpose of democratising the news landscape by preventing it from falling in any one hand or one big business house.

The bill never saw the light of day, but the news landscape had changed for all times to come. Subsequent attempts made by successive governments to regulate news have been met with resistance by the media itself.

In 2006-07, another attempt was made to revisit the Broadcast Bill,[2] but this exercise got mired in a controversy over attempts to regulate and control news. The Congress-led United Progressive Alliance (UPA) government was seen as muzzling freedom of expression and given the past record of the party, especially in a study mapping the digital media landscape undertaken by Open

1. *http://www.outlookindia.com/printarticle.aspx?204133*

2. *http://mib.nic.in/ShowDocs.aspx*

Forum, where I was part of a team, we found, that as of 2011—of the 745 channels which had been granted the licence to operate—366 were news channels. Such is the craze for operating and consuming news. One of the reasons was the transponder costs had crashed. As Khandekar writes, "the crash $3 million in the beginning of the 90s to $200,000 opened the gates for anyone wanting to run a channel." To add to this, the advertising market had also opened up and television gobbled up a lion's share of the advertising market. But how many of the owners are known to the viewing public? Or for that matter, how many channels are run by politicians and political parties are operational in the country? How does news reflect the views of their owners and how objective and fair is the news? Is the viewer aware of who calls the tune?

Ownership

Before we come to the issue of ownership of news, it is pertinent to point out here that the producers of news for Doordarshan like NDTV and Living Media became news broadcasters in their own right. Or for that matter, the anchor of the immensely popular Aap Ki Adalat, a mock court trial of celebrities, Rajat Sharma, went on to start his own channel, India TV which remains one of the few marketing successes in news history. What spurred them to start on their own? Perhaps, a climate had already been created for news, and advertisers were willing to advertise on news. The economies of running a news channel were not cheap, although one could cut down costs too by not investing in fresh programming. But of that, later.

Broadly, ownership of print and television falls into the following categories: channels owned by politicians; political parties who own channels; and corporates who own or have stake in media houses and government-owned channels. The Hoot, a website, tracked down political parties and governments who own channels—a work in progress. Political parties owning media, print and television is nothing new. In a series of articles, authors Paranjoy Guha Thakurta and Aditi Roy Ghatak, write that from the undivided Communist party which had Langol and then Swadhinta, owning the media was crucial to the dissemination of views and the party position. They state:

> Today, the Communist Party of India (CPI) (Marxist) is quite a media conglomerate at a national level. Its central organs are People's Democracy in English, from New Delhi, Kolkata, Kochi, Hyderabad, and Agartala, and the Lok Lehar in Hindi. The Party publishes a theoretical quarterly, The Marxist; five dailies in different Indian languages; several weeklies and fortnightlies in Assamese, Oriya, Bengali, Malayalam, Punjabi, Kannada, Marathi, and Gujarati. Its Hindi weekly, Swadhinata, and its Urdu fortnightly, Abshar, are published from Kolkata. Besides, there are Janashakti (Kannada), Jeevan Marg (Marathi), Samyabadi (Oriya), Ganashakti (Assamese and Bengali) and Chitan (Gujarati). There are also Hindi fortnightlies, Lok Samvad (Uttar Pradesh), Lok Jatan (Madhya Pradesh), and Lok Janvad (Bihar). These efforts are backed by its own news agency, the India News Network. The party also runs a publishing house, Left Word Books, which deals in broad Left-wing publications only. That apart, it has publishing houses in various States such as the National Book Agency in West Bengal, the Chinta Publications in Kerala, and the Prajashakti Book House in Andhra Pradesh.[3]

In Tamil Nadu, which has always seen governance by either the All India Anna Dravida Munnetra Kazhagam (AIADMK) or the DMK, the media too finds itself neatly owned by these parties. Kalanithi Maran, the grand nephew of DMK chief Karunanidhi, controls virtually the entire media landscape in Tamil Nadu. Sun TV, Sun News, Sun TV, Sumangali cable (which distributes the channels), KTV, Udaya and newspapers *Dinakaran* and Red FM 93.5. After the Marans split from Karunanidhi, the patriarch of the party started the Kalaignar TV Private Limited. But political ownership of the media was not confined to one or two states. As The Hoot article showed, politicians and political parties in virtually all the states had started their own media platforms.

From ownership to exertions from owners, in an article I wrote in *Outlook*, back in 2011,[4] I examined how politicians had become

3. *http://www.thehoot.org/web/storypage/6046-1-1-4-true.html*
4. *http://www.outlookindia.com/article/Their-Masters-Image/270727*

de facto editors of publications and television channels. From taking part in editorial meetings, to remote control of news selection, to having trusted lieutenants to do their bidding news, became malleable in the owner's hands.

All that was required to start a news channel was ₹100-odd crores, and with the Telecom Regulatory Authority of India (TRAI) reducing the net worth of political parties who wanted to run a news channel to ₹15 crore from the earlier ₹100 crores, it is easy to guess why politicians/political parties jumped in the fray.

In Andhra Pradesh, there are 14 news channels owned or partially bankrolled by politicians. In Karnataka, there are four, and in Tamil Nadu five. Kerala, West Bengal, Maharashtra and Uttar Pradesh have their fair share of channels linked to politicians. There are about 40 news channels which are either funded by political parties or directly owned by politicians.

Of the dozen or so Bengali news channels, 24 Ghanta is pro-CPI(M), and Channel 10 and Kolkata TV are pro-Trinamool Congress. In fact, it is not uncommon to hear the viewer saying, "oh this channel belongs to CPM." While those who work in these channels denied any direct interference, there is no denying that the channels serve as a mouthpiece for the party. It was primarily to counter the channel that Mamata Banerjee's TMC decided to start of its own. Says Partha Chatterjee of the TMC, "Certain channels have ceased to be looked upon as reliable sources of unbiased news. But television channels have reach and so we need to counter the effect their campaigning will have on us. This is why we decided to start our own channel" (Their Master's Image, *Outlook*, 2011).

The channels function as a mouthpiece for the parties, in power and those out of it, and content lacks objectivity. As we found out while writing the article in *Outlook*, the guiding principle for news in channels is: 'Praise the leader'.

How often does the viewer discern the difference between news and propaganda. How often has the viewer asked why is a channel or newspaper they read plugging for a politician? The question is pertinent and the more I engaged with it, I found news is seldom objective. Allow me to digress a bit and get back to the story of RIL-owned Network 18. This was a complicated business entanglement that began with an advance from a trust owned by RIL to the Raghav Bahl-owned Network 18, to pick up a stake in the Andhra Pradesh-based Ramoji Rao's Eenadu network. Essentially, Bahl was picking up RIL's own stake in Eenadu, which was a secret until revealed in a complicated litigation process. The reasons for RIL's stake in Eenadu were quite transparent. Compelling political reasons made the deal possible and this time Mukesh Ambani was facing flak for his 2G gas basin. It was convergence of corporate, media and political interests as Rao was close to Telegu Desam Party's (TDP) N. Chandrababu Naidu, now in alliance with the Bharatiya Janata Party (BJP).

As the monthly *Caravan* in its December 2014 issue, notes:

> In some way, Rao ambitions and his position, remain undiminished today. His talent for political friendships has endured. This summer, dressed in habitual white safari suit, he sat in the front row of the audience at the swearing-in ceremony of Prime Minister Narendra Modi at Rashtrapati Bhavan, alongside the heads of Pakistan, Afghanistan and Bhutan. Andhra Pradesh's chief minister Chandrababu Naidu, sat in the row behind him. Rao had met Modi in Ahmedabad before the general election, than to the effort of another mutual friend, Venkaiah Naidu. In the aftermath of the 2002 riots in Gujarat, bulletins in ETV Gujarati had largely been charitable to then chief minister Modi. During the 2014 election campaign, Modi visited Ramoji Film City and granted his first interview of the campaign, speaking in Hindi, to the ETV network.

Increasingly, the lines between politics, business and media are getting blurred. As business interests converge. The media requires money. The corporates are the only ones with deep pockets. It's not as if the corporate alone exercise control over the media. Governments too exert pressure through advertisements—the classic carrot and stick method—deployed to ask the media to mend its ways. Witness what happened in Kashmir when newspapers critical of the Centre encountered an advertisement freeze. The papers had a tough time to print matter.

the Kumarmangalam Birla group—does the average reader know the reasons why? Or when news channel Headlines Today, does not lead with the same, does the reader know that Birla has a stake in the television company? Or, when newspapers in Madhya Pradesh do not write about a mining group, is the reader aware that they are owned by one? It is in this context that ownership of news assumes importance and as interests converge, the viewers and the readers must know who the suppliers of news are.

As Paranjoy Guha Thakurta notes in *The Hoot*:

> As already stated, in India and in the world, large media corporations are today clearly playing a bigger role in the political economy that they report on as a result of forward and backward linkages. (The dominance in Italy's media of companies controlled by Silvio Berlusconi, that country's longest serving head of government, is a case in point.) In this country, large international television broadcast networks including Turner/CNN, Viacom/MTV and Sony are acquiring or partnering regional networks. Moreover, a fair degree of consolidation and convergence has already taken place.

Who can forget the embarrassment in the media, not to mention the political fallout, following the Radia tapes controversy—I quote from the study I had taken part in.

> The Radia tapes comprising of telephone conversations that Niira Radia, an independent lobbyist handling PR and government liaison for leading business groups such as Tata and Mukesh Ambani, had with dozens of renowned television and print journalists, politicians, bureaucrats, and other lobbyists. A few of these conversations were with Ms Barkha Dutt, Group Editor at NDTV, and Vir Sanghvi, then Editorial Director of the Hindustan Times, who was subsequently re-designated as Advisor. Dutt came across as a journalist who seemed to be acting as a "messenger" for discussions on the selection of cabinet ministers between two of the ruling coalition partners just after the national elections in May 2009. Mr Sanghvi, in contrast, discussed details of his forthcoming column(s) with Radia in a bid to convince her that the contents were spun in favor of one of her clients, Mukesh Ambani. Much later, Mr Sanghvi said that his conversations were "doctored"; even the government argued in the Supreme Court that the tapes were tampered with. The Supreme Court has still not given a judgment.

The conversations revealed how embedded the media was with the establishment.

Is the Quality of News Taking a Hit?

In the backdrop of consolidation and takeover, is there a dumbing down of news? While the days of advertising superstition on Hindi channels are over, there is pressure on keeping time-slots for horoscope reading. Less and less investment is being made in news-gathering. There is more and more pressure to do what the leader does. A leading anchor tells me, "we just have to follow news breaks if Times Now breaks it first." Incidentally, Times Now is the leader of the pack with a 24 per cent market share in the English news segment. Has news become an entertainment with a babble of voices producing noise? How seriously is the news consumed? The answers to these questions cannot be quantified. What we do have are Television Audience Measurement (TAM) figures for news viewership. But given the fact that there are only a little over 11,000 metres to cover 60 per cent of the population, the viewership becomes suspect. There is pressure on TV to run with a story and often, the consequences can be disastrous—as English channel Times Now found to its dismay. In September 2008, Times Now ran a story about a provident fund scam involving judges and wrongly included the photograph of a nationally well-known judge, who had nothing to do with it—an incident that the senior manager of the channel is quoted to have attributed to "the obsession with speed. Though Times Now aired a correction, albeit 15 days later, and an apology two days subsequently, the dissatisfied judge filed a suit in a local court."

Again quoting from the study mentioned above: "In December 2010, The Hindu reported about an ethical breach that involved the English news channel CNN-IBN and the tweets it aired for a prime-time program on "should lobbying be legalised?" Later, the channel apologised to its viewers on its website'.

There is pressure on news organisations to run with the news without even the elementary diligence and/or confirmation, largely because of the speed prompted by digitisation and increased competition.

It is the same speed that has led to the breaking news phenomenon—which has more to do with besting rivals. Are full disclosures a way out and if so, how will this be implemented and mandated? If, for example leading daily *Times of India* which has a joint venture with *Huffington Post*—carries an interview with the CEO of the Post—Arraina Huffington without disclosing they are in a joint pact, does this amount to breach of trust? On the other hand, newspapers like *the Mint* carry disclosures when they write stories on rival business newspapers. Some newspapers like the *Indian Express* have evolved practices which include asking their reporters to declare in a sealed envelope, their investments in companies. The reporters are prohibited from reporting on corporates if they have invested in shares. Similarly, when editors have stakes in companies which run their newspapers, they should come out clean. A leading media critic who has a two per cent stake in a business daily, writes a column for its rival business paper. An year ago, the Editor's Guild had proposed a full-disclosure policy that required editors to declare all their wealth. It had few takers. Shouldn't the unsuspecting reader know this fact?

Shouldn't the viewer know why CNN-IBN in 2008—in the backdrop of the trust vote against Manmohan Singh government on the nuclear issue—promised an expose on the—money-for-vote scam but never did? No reasons were given for shelving the expose. Come election time, it is very difficult to spot whether an interview by a politician is paid for or sponsored. It is equally difficult to know whether the politician is on the board of the media company. What is the way ahead for news in an era of convergence? It is not only a convergence in the media, but also that of interests as the media, politician and the businessman become bedfellows. These are the questions which require an examination for best practices to evolve.

Section III

Regional Surge

5

K.S. ARUL SELVAN*

TV News Scenario in South India

National channels receive the least viewership in south India, as small sections of population in these states are familiar with the English language and contrary to northern India, Hindi is not the popular choice of television medium, particularly for news consumption. The vacuum created by low popularity of leading English and Hindi news channels in these regions, along with the diverse features of cultural, political, economic conditions, has provided ample space for regional language news channels to flourish in the respective states.

Table 5.1

Channel Genre-wise Share (2009 versus 2010)

	All India		*Hindi Market*		*South*	
	2009	*2010*	*2009*	*2010*	*2009*	*2010*
Regional News	3.7	3.7	2.3	2.2	6.3	6.9
Hindi news	3.6	3.4	5.3	5.0	0.3	0.2
English news	0.4	0.3	0.3	0.3	0.5	0.4

Source: TAM Analysis.

In the overall viewership to television, viewership to news genre has declined marginally between 2009 and 2010, according to TAM's (television audience measurement) own analysis. Viewership to regional news channels, however, remained at 3.7 both in 2009 and 2010. In the south, share of regional news channels in the overall viewership had gone up from 6.3 to 6.9 between 2009 and 2010.

* Inputs from P.N. Vasanti.

National and state elections in the recent past has created enormous platform for many stakeholders to start news channels. Many players have changed their business patterns, and new channels entered the highly competitive area with new objectives and approaches. As per information posted the Ministry of Information & Broadcasting (I&B) of Government of India (GoI) on November 2014, there are 821 television channels with an approval to operate in India, out of which 404 channels are dedicated to news and current affairs. In all, nearly 41 television news channels exist in the five South Indian languages. In that, Telugu leads in terms of highest number of news channels.

Scope and structure of news channels in Tamil, Telugu, Malayalam and Kannada has been distinct from the very outset. Over the years, the numbers have multiplied much faster and the key movers mostly are political leaders and businessmen. The ownership patterns of television news channels of south India, shows three associated distinct patterns in the respective language based states. These patterns are: a) ownership by political parties or people/groups affiliated to parties; b) ownership by people or groups of a leading business ventures; and c) ownership by the journalists or news organisations.

Political ownership and affiliation is most obvious in south Indian language news channels. Tamil leads the race of political ownership of television medium particularly news channels. Observations made by *Forbes* (2012) kind of sums up TN news channels' scenario: "Tamil Nadu has the most balanced media in the whole of India, a long-standing joke in the state went, only, you have to watch two channels to achieve that balance. To know how bad DMK is, watch Jaya, and to know how bad AIADMK is, watch Sun".

However, in other languages of south India, news channels are closely associated with specific channels—a leading Bharatiya Janata Party (BJP) member of the Parliament has investment in Survarna and Asianet, T News prefers TRS party and Telengana news compared to others. Two channels of Telugu—10TV and 99%TV—has close links with the Communist parties. The communist party in Kerala too is officially part of a few of the channels.

In TN, individual channels are part of major parties, which even the audience can figure out while watching the news. Major channels that claim to be independent have a tacit link with established parties.

Box 5.1

*Party Associated Channels**

Kannada

1. Kasthuri News: Owner is wife of Janata Dal (S) politician.
2. Udaya News: Owner closely associated with the Tamil Nadu politics.

Malayalam

1. Indiavision: Associated with the Indian Muslim League party.
2. People TV: Associated with CPI (M).

Tamil

1. SUN News: Group's owner is son of former Cabinet Minister, brother of former Cabinet Minister, and grandson of former Chief Minister of Tamil Nadu.
2. Kalaignar Seithigal: Jointly owned by wife and daughter of former Chief Minister of Tamil Nadu.
3. Jaya TV News: Group has close affiliation with the AIADMK. Channel uses election symbol of this party.
4. Makkal TV: Owned by PMK.
5. Captain News: Owned by DMDK.
6. Vasanth TV & Mega TV: Owned by Congress state functionaries.

Telugu

1. Sakshi TV (2009): YSR Congress owns this channel.
2. Gemini News: Owner closely associated with the Tamil Nadu and Andhra politics.

Note: * These are indicative as many channels, investors and funding sources are not available.

Source: Compiled from multiple sources.

The second pattern of ownership involves business corporations. Independent companies are established to run news channels—some of them with backing from mining barons, real estate magnates and political leaders of major parties, they are the business interest groups behind establishing channels in South Indian news channels.

A Telugu news channel, 10 TV, became the first Telugu channel to be launched as a cooperative venture, which is funded by the people.

Few initiatives are also taken by eminent journalists and media houses. Thanthi TV in Tamil, Manorama and Mathrubhoomi News in Malayalam and ETV News and ABN Andhra Jyoti in Telugu have a common feature—these channels were established by the leading newspapers of Tamil, Malayalam and Telugu languages. Contrary to that, BTV and Public TV in Kannada were established by the leading independent journalists of Karnataka.

The ongoing debate on southern regional channels is on their open and public stand with their respective political affiliations, including using their broadcast time to give enormous space for its political leaders and party. Particularly during the election time, these channels give live coverage of speeches delivered by their respective party leaders. Both the ethical and legal implications of such affiliations and ownership patterns are often discussed and written about. On the other hand, the trend of 'paid news', or 'paid ratings', and the like, have come to the fore apparently because of increased involvement of political leaders and business people in the ownership or/and management of channels, and more number of media persons are becoming active in electoral politics, directly and indirectly.

The Case of Telugu Channels

A cut-throat competition is prevailing in Telugu television news industry. Network-based news channels are quite popular here—Network 18 backed ETV news, SUN network supported Gemini news, and TV9 network owns TV9 Telugu. Raj News, which is a media group based in Tamil, also owns channels in Telugu (as well as in other South Indian languages too). Although channels are not owned directly by the political parties, there are channels which are maintained by the leaders of major political parties of Telangana, as well as AP. Apart from these two major ownership patterns, there are company-owned as well as newspaper-owned channels.

There were 17 news channels in Telugu in 2012 and 19 in 2014. Six more have already been permitted. Telugu news channels tend to have two or three distinct categories of news bulletins in the course of the day: one being a 'news bulletin' with a mix of national and state news and the other being a mix of state and local news. The third news bulletin is 'primarily local' with extensive and reflective field coverage of the districts across the state, however briefly it may be, but always footage based. This, apparently, is a lesson that the Telugu news channels have picked up—good camaraderie with Telugu news dailies, which has expanded their very relevance as well as reach by having 'district editions' for most districts of the state.

Perhaps, there is no parallel in any other state where a GEC Channel (MAA) discontinued broadcasting two or three news bulletins a day, despite the group not having any other 24x7 news channel. This is also contrary to CMS study (2007-2009) insights on viewership. It reveals that the channel which telecast news bulletins twice or thrice a day have better chances of being viewed more seriously compared to round the clock news channels.

List of Telugu Language Channels

a. 10TV—the channel is owned through a cooperative way of investment and is open for audience to invest in/own the channel. The channel was launched in 2013, and promoted by the Spoorthi Communications Pvt. Ltd. (*http://www.10tv.in*).

b. 99% TV—a Telugu news channel. (*http://www.99tvtelugu.com*).

c. ABN Andhra Jyoti—the channel is owned and operated by the Amoda Broadcasting Network. The other sister media concern is Telugu daily *Andhra Jyoti*, which started its news broadcast in 2009 (*http://www.abnandhrajyothy.com*).

d. CVR News—a 24x7 Telugu channel launched in 2011, owned by Image Broadcasting Private Limited. (*http://www.cvrnews.tv*).

e. ETV Telugu News—ETV was part of Ramoji Rao's banquet of channels earlier, but now it is a part of TV18—a Reliance subsidiary. It started its operations from 2003. In 2010, the ETV network had added another channel to cater to

Telangana, and the earlier channel was renamed as ETV Andhra Pradesh. (*http://etv2.etv.co.in*).

f. Gemini News—the channel is part of Kalanidhi Maran's SUN Network. This Telugu news service had begun from 2004.

g. HMTV—a Telugu 24x7 news channel owned by the Hyderabad Media House. The channel is functioning since 2008. (*http://www.hmtvlive.com*).

h. NTV—NTV stands for Next Generation TV; it started its broadcasting in 2007. Channel is owned by Rachana Television Private Limited. The group also owns a devotional channel, Bhakti TV and a channel for women, Vanitha TV (*http://www.ntvtelugu.com*).

i. Raj News Telugu—Raj TV network has news channels in all four languages of south India—Kannada (2009), Malayalam (2009), Tamil (2007) and Telugu (2007) (*http://rajtv.tv/News/NEWS.aspx*).

j. Sakshi TV—channel belongs to Sakshi media group owned by Y.S. Jaganmohan Reddy, President of YSR Congress. Channel was launched in 2009 (*http://www.sakshitv.com*).

k. StudioN—channel owned by the Narne Networks Pvt. Ltd., started its broadcast 2008 onwards (*http://www.studiononline.com*).

l. Tnews—Telugu channel meant for Telangana state, launched in 2011 (*http://www.tnewslive.com*).

m. TV 5 News—a Telugu channel that had started its news services in 2007, owned by Shreya Broadcasting Pvt. Ltd. (*http://www.tv5news.in*).

n. TV9 Telugu—This is a 24x7 Telugu channel, owned by the Associated Broadcasting Company Pvt. Ltd. (ABCl), it started its broadcast from mid-2004. The ABCl owns network of many channels, including news channels as well in Telugu, Gujarati and Marathi (*http://www.tv9.com/Tv9-andhrapradesh/home_tel.htm*).

o. V6 News—VIL Media Pvt. Ltd. owns this channel; it had started its operations in 2012 (*http://v6news.tv*).

Tamil News Channels

Business operations of Tamil news channels follow a very simple arithmetic. Each popular political parties as part of their routine set-up, has created channels for themselves. Major investment comes from their respective parties and fund flow is constant here. Although SUN news network claims to be independent in their news selection and delivery, there are marked differences in their coverage of Dravida Munnetra Kazhagam (DMK) and rest of the political parties. SUN network is India's leading publicly listed media company in India. It owns a wide variety of channels cutting across all four South Indian languages. However, in news segment, SUN news in Tamil has got greater popular reach in comparison to other channels like Udaya News in Kannada, and Gemini News in Telugu.

Another big network of media channels is owned by DMK itself—Kalaignar groups of channels. Other political parties, like AIADMK, too have scores of channels. There are also two channels meant for National Congress. Funding for these network channels or individual channels comes from respective parties.

However, what appears as a classic case of lack of objectivity is simply a business proposition for a group of media networks that became successful simply by taking a neutral stand in Tamil television news arena. Puthiya Thalaimurai was established in 2011, the channel is owned by an educational group of company. This channel is leading the ranking list of Tamil news channels for the past three years. Their success model is based on taking an objective stand and not siding with any political party.

List of Tamil Language Channels

a. Captain News—Desiya Murpokku Dravida Kazhagam's President and Tamil actor Vijayakant's brother-in-law owns this channel. This channel started its news broadcast in 2012. This group also owns a general entertainment channel, Captain TV (*http://captainnews.net*).

b. Jaya Plus News—channel belongs to AIADMK, and uses party election symbol as a logo. Started its broadcast from 2004. (*http://jayanewslive.com*).

d. Mathrubhumi News—Like the previous entry, this channel too is owned by the leading Malayalam dialy *Mathrubhumi*. This channel has started its broadcasting from 2013 (*http://mathrubhuminews.in/ee/home/index*).
e. People TV—It is owned by the Malayalam Communications Limited; film actor, Mamoorty is the channel's Chairman and the CPI (M) has shares in it (*www.peopletvonline.com*).
f. Reporter TV—Started in 2011 by the Indo Asian News Channel Pvt Ltd (*http://reporterlive.com*).
g. TV New—The channel started its operation from 2011 onwards and is owned by various Kerala-based business people through Kerala Chamber of Commerce and Industry (*http://tvnew.in*).

Kannada News Channels

The first Kannada satellite news channel, Udaya TV, was launched in 1994. Then, the year 2006 saw the entry of TV9 Kannada, which went on to become a leading channel with the highest TRP rankings. The news channel is owned by Ravi Prakash of Sneha TV network, a group from Hyderabad which also owns news channels in AP, Kerala, Madhya Pradesh (MP), Uttar Pradesh (UP), Maharashtra, and other states.

In Karnataka, most of the news channels have direct or indirect relations with politicians. Kasthuri News 24, launched by the wife of leader H.D. Kumarswamy, Anita Kumarswamy, is one such TV channel that reflects that politics play a crucial role in Kannada television news industry. Suvarna News 24x7, in which Rajeev Chandrasekhar has a stake and Samaya TV owned by Murugesh Nirani, are other examples.

This is not to say that Kannada viewers have very limited choice of getting neutral/objective news from these news channels. There are channels managed independently by leading journalists too. Public TV, a 24-hour Kannada language news television channel launched on 26 January 2012 by veteran journalist H. Rangnath (former anchor of Suvarna News), heightened the debate on the rising number of channels in the state and intensified competition for TRPs among the competitors. He also raised the bar of transparency by declaring his assets live on television—perhaps a unique initiative by a TV media owner in India. However, this competition has led to a rise in sensational coverage with more doses of crime, sex and scandals on TV News. Overall, it has decreased content quality and credibility of Kannada television news channels.

An instance of news channels getting in trouble for sensational coverage was in May 2014, when the Karnataka High Court had to step in and issue notices to Kannada news channels Suvarna TV, TV 9, Samaya TV, Kasthuri TV, Janashri, ETV and Public TV for repeatedly broadcasting CCTV footage of godman Devishree Ramaswamy in a compromising position with women.

Kannada Language Channels

a. BTV News—Mooted by various journalists in 2014.
b. ETV News—ETV was part of Ramoji Rao's banquet of channels earlier, now it is part of TV18—a Reliance subsidiary (*www.news18.com/live-tv/etv-kannada*).
c. Janasri—The channel is owned by the mining barons, Reddy brothers of Bellary of Karnataka. One of the owners, G. Janardhan Reddy was arrested by Central Bureau of Investigation (CBI) (*www.janasritv.com*).
d. Kasthuri News—The channel is owned by former Chief Minister of Karnataka H.D. Kumaraswamy of Janata Dal (Secular) party. Kumaraswamy's father H. Deva Gowda was former Prime Minister of India. It started its news broadcast from 2007 (*www.kasthuritv.com*).
e. Public TV—It is an initiative of a journalist and the broadcast has begun from 2012 (*www.publictv.in*).
f. Raj News—This channel is part of TN based Raj Television Network, owned by Raajhendhran. It started its operation from 2013 (*www.rajkanada.in*).
g. Suvarna News—It is owned by the Asianet group, started its operations in 2008. The Channel is owned by MP Rajeev Chandrasekhar. He also owns *Kannada Prabha*, a daily newspaper (*www.suvarnanews.tv*).

h. TV9 Kannada—This is a 24x7 Kannada channel, owned by the ABCl; it started its broadcast from 2006. The ABCl owns network of many channels, including news channels in Telugu, Gujarati and Marathi (*www.tv9.com/tv9-bangalore/index.html*).
i. Udaya Varthegalu—The channel is part of Kalanidhi Maran's SUN Network, started Kannada service from 2006 (no dedicated website).

News Content Pattern

Regional news channels, unlike Hindi and English ones, which position themselves as 'national', devote far more time in originating news in a competitive spirit and have far better range in the subjects covered. Relatively, regional language news channels are far more focused, reflective and inclusive in their coverage than those of national news channels.

An analysis of CMS Media Lab reports shows that Telugu news channels' coverage is almost live with news from across the state, from different regions and far-off places. They are much better in covering the real 'issues of concern' and reflecting voice of many more. They do so with more regularity than the national news channels. Telugu news channels cover rural AP more extensively and regularly, not only with special news programmes, but also in the normal course of news bulletins. Such an extensive coverage of rural areas, farmers and grass roots is perhaps because television set ownership ratio in AP is greater than in the case of the rural Hindi belt. It is also because of competition with Telugu newspapers and political business interests of news channels. The analysis of news channel coverage in Hindi, English and Telugu implies that the Hindi news channel bulletins are relatively more ratings driven than the Telugu ones. Nevertheless, the content model followed by Telugu news channels are also by and large ratings motivated.

Regional news channels have consolidated by increasing state-specific coverage, including that of districts and beyond urban areas. For example, news channels in Telugu (particularly ETV 2 and TV9 news) increased such content from one-third before 2000 to more than half in 2010. And, simultaneously, Delhi centric news declined significantly during the period. This certainly helped regional channels to expand their reach and facilitated competition in covering grass roots with a wide range of topics.

In general, politics, crime and entertainment are the staple food of South Indian language television news channels. A Telugu news channel became popular by exposing the sex scandal of a former state Governor and a Tamil channel is known for publicising the sex tape of a religious leader. Apart from these focus areas of regional channels, in general, the prime time news is primarily dominated by state politics news, major incidents of crime across the state and various entertainment live telecast—particularly by the SUN network's live coverage of IPL cricket matches.

Prime time discussion oriented programmes are visible across all language channels. In the evening, just prior to prime time news, an adequate coverage of state news round-up is a regular feature. Daytime news is dominated by business news and investment tracking based discussions. Special episodes on sports are also common featured in the non-prime time slots.

A overview analysis of the programme schedule of few television news channels across the language broadcast reveals that the channels focus primarily on presenting current events promptly throughout the day with the help of newsfeed from agencies and own news production by means of using technology extensively, including few live coverage of events around the state including film award shows, press meets, seminars and also weddings of famous personalities. Secondly, during the prime time, a majority of the channels hosts discussion-oriented programme on that day's major events. Business news is common in the morning slot until noon, and international and sports news are visible in the evening schedule, just before prime time broadcast. Entertainment, specifically cinema news, is noticed across the board. Many channels give importance to religious content and yoga in the early morning slots. There is a marked difference between weekday and weekend programmes—more of current developments in weekdays, and analysis-oriented documentaries and news packages are part of weekends. Channels backed by newspapers and journalists have wider variety than those owned by business groups.

Majority of these regional language channels operate their dedicated web presence by presenting news in textual format along with the necessary video clippings. Besides, the Kannada media's web presence is coupled with live streaming of their regular broadcasts. Through web presence, these channels primarily target two kinds of audience—one to their language diaspora and secondly to ones who migrate out of their native state but has settled in other parts of India. Apart from websites, many regional language broadcasts and its contents are available through specially created 'Apps' or applications.

In summary, the southern language news channels are currently a vibrant and yet widely debated space. This is also currently the place where serious innovation and experimentation with news formats, genre, bulletins, etc., in television news are being attempted. The overall political, social and economical implications of these channels need to be studied seriously for a better understanding of such unique phenomenon.

References

FICCI-KPMG. (2013). "Indian Media and Entertainment Industry Report 2014". Retrived 2 December 2014 from *https://www.kpmg.com/IN/en/Topics/FICCI-Frames/Documents/FICCI-Frames-2014-The-stage-is-set-Report-2014.pdf*

Indiantelevision.com (2010). "TV News Consumption in the South". Retrived 22 November 2014 from *http://www.indiantelevision.com/special/y2k10/south news_yearender.php*

Ministry of I&B (2014). *List of Permitted Private Satellite Channels*. Retrived 3 December 2014 from *http://mib.nic.in/WriteReadData/documents/List_of_Permitted Private_Satellite_TV_Channels_as_on_30-11-2014.pdf*

Ram, N. (2011). "The Changing Role of the News Media in Contemporary India". Retrived 2 December 2014 from *http://www.thehindu.com/multimedia/archive/00863/Contemporary_India__863821a.pdf*

Ramnath, N.S. (2012). "New Competition for Tamil Nadu TV Channels", *Forbes India Magazine*. Retrived 3 December 2014 from *http://forbesindia.com/printcontent/33040*.

Ranganathan, Maya (2012). "TV Politics in Tamil Nadu", *Thehoot.org*. 10 September. Retrived 21 November 2014 from *http://thehoot.org/web/TV-politics-in-Tamil-Nadu/6249-1-1-2-true.html*

Batabyal, Somnath (2010) "Constructing an Audience: News Television Practices in India", *Contemporary South Asia* 18(4): 387-399.

Tilak, G. Sudha. (2012). "Tamil Nadu's TV Empires", *Newslaundry.com*. 12 September. Retrived 22 November 2014 from *http://www.newslaundry.com/2012/09/24/tamil-nadus-tv-empires/*

The Newsminute.com (2014). "All you wanted to know about who owns the South Indian news channels you watch". Retrived 26 November from *http://www.thenewsminute.com/news_sections/1772*

news declined significantly during the period. This certainly helped regional channels to expand their reach and facilitated competition in covering grass roots with a wide range of topics.

In general, politics, crime and entertainment are the staple food of South Indian language television news channels. A Telugu news channel became popular by exposing the sex scandal of a former state Governor and a Tamil channel is known for publicising the sex tape of a religious leader. Apart from these focus areas of regional channels, in general, the prime time news is primarily dominated by state politics news, major incidents of crime across the state and various entertainment live telecast—particularly by the SUN network's live coverage of IPL cricket matches.

Prime time discussion oriented programmes are visible across all language channels. In the evening, just prior to prime time news, an adequate coverage of state news round-up is a regular feature. Daytime news is dominated by business news and investment tracking based discussions. Special episodes on sports are also common featured in the non-prime time slots.

A overview analysis of the programme schedule of few television news channels across the language broadcast reveals that the channels focus primarily on presenting current events promptly throughout the day with the help of newsfeed from agencies and own news production by means of using technology extensively, including few live coverage of events around the state including film award shows, press meets, seminars and also weddings of famous personalities. Secondly, during the prime time, a majority of the channels hosts discussion-oriented programme on that day's major events. Business news is common in the morning slot until noon, and international and sports news are visible in the evening schedule, just before prime time broadcast. Entertainment, specifically cinema news, is noticed across the board. Many channels give importance to religious content and yoga in the early morning slots. There is a marked difference between weekday and weekend programmes—more of current developments in weekdays, and analysis-oriented documentaries and news packages are part of weekends. Channels backed by newspapers and journalists have wider variety than those owned by business groups.

Majority of these regional language channels operate their dedicated web presence by presenting news in textual format along with the necessary video clippings. Besides, the Kannada media's web presence is coupled with live streaming of their regular broadcasts. Through web presence, these channels primarily target two kinds of audience—one to their language diaspora and secondly to ones who migrate out of their native state but has settled in other parts of India. Apart from websites, many regional language broadcasts and its contents are available through specially created 'Apps' or applications.

In summary, the southern language news channels are currently a vibrant and yet widely debated space. This is also currently the place where serious innovation and experimentation with news formats, genre, bulletins, etc., in television news are being attempted. The overall political, social and economical implications of these channels need to be studied seriously for a better understanding of such unique phenomenon.

References

FICCI-KPMG. (2013). "Indian Media and Entertainment Industry Report 2014". Retrived 2 December 2014 from *https://www.kpmg.com/IN/en/Topics/FICCI-Frames/Documents/FICCI-Frames-2014-The-stage-is-set-Report-2014.pdf*

Indiantelevision.com (2010). "TV News Consumption in the South". Retrived 22 November 2014 from *http://www.indiantelevision.com/special/y2k10/south news_yearender.php*

Ministry of I&B (2014). *List of Permitted Private Satellite Channels*. Retrived 3 December 2014 from *http://mib.nic.in/WriteReadData/documents/List_of_Permitted Private_Satellite_TV_Channels_as_on_30-11-2014.pdf*

Ram, N. (2011). "The Changing Role of the News Media in Contemporary India". Retrived 2 December 2014 from *http://www.thehindu.com/multimedia/archive/00863/Contemporary_India__863821a.pdf*

Ramnath, N.S. (2012). "New Competition for Tamil Nadu TV Channels", *Forbes India Magazine*. Retrived 3 December 2014 from *http://forbesindia.com/printcontent/33040*.

Ranganathan, Maya (2012). "TV Politics in Tamil Nadu", *Thehoot.org*. 10 September. Retrived 21 November 2014 from *http://thehoot.org/web/TV-politics-in-Tamil-Nadu/6249-1-1-2-true.html*

Batabyal, Somnath (2010) "Constructing an Audience: News Television Practices in India", *Contemporary South Asia* 18(4): 387-399.

Tilak, G. Sudha. (2012). "Tamil Nadu's TV Empires", *Newslaundry.com*. 12 September. Retrived 22 November 2014 from *http://www.newslaundry.com/2012/09/24/tamil-nadus-tv-empires/*

The Newsminute.com (2014). "All you wanted to know about who owns the South Indian news channels you watch". Retrived 26 November from *http://www.thenewsminute.com/news_sections/1772*

6

MRINAL TALUKDAR

TV News in Northeast India

Almost every journalist in India knows that the most happening place for news in the last few decades have been Kashmir and Northeast India. Simply because conflict brings news.

Insurgency, influence of neighbouring countries and overdose of emotions have always kept Northeast India in the limelight for the media of mainland India. Media has always thrived for the Northeast, but that of the region has a long way to go.

Northeast India is a curious case, where television technology raced ahead of trained manpower, resulting in a half-baked immature media, often creating havoc in states like Assam.

In the actual terms of media as a whole, the Northeast India has not matured well enough to be compared with the rest of India. Technically, most of the states have improved but yet there are miles to go before a professional independent character is profoundly evident.

Assam has technology but not the manpower. Rest of the Northeast is suffering from both. Consequently, the Northeast remains undercovered in their own media. Again, media of Assam is generally interpretative laced with agenda journalism, while rest of the region is more or less objective. Assam boasts five 24x7 satellite news channels, but none of them are purely news channels as more than 30 per cent content are film, songs and tele-serials.

The seven states of the region can be divided in three broad divisions.

In the first group, there is only Assam, which is way ahead than the other states in television journalism with five satellite news channels, beside three other separate entertainment channels. But their news content is increasingly getting interpretative as traditional journalism has been completely discarded for sensational journalism. The things are taking a turn for worse as lack of trained manpower has forced the channels to change the character of journalism.

In the second group, we can place Manipur, Tripura and Mizoram where the electronic media has started evolving. Both Mizoram and Tripura have their own satellite channels, but Manipur has two well-organised cable television channels with a wider reach. All the three states have attempted serious journalism and comparatively, news content is objective and better than Assam; it is also not driven by political agenda. However, all three are handicapped by the lack of technology, finance, manpower and small footprint.

In the third group, remain Meghalaya, Arunachal Pradesh and Nagaland, where there are only local cable networks and no satellite channels. The media has not come up to a professional level in order to influence the society and bring probity to public life. The cable network just covers the events of their area and broadcasts it.

Although, the region is unquestionably newsy, it has never been the cradle of strong professional journalism. There have been occasional flash of brilliances producing great journalists, but backwardness of the region, coupled with government dependent economy, has never allowed the media to grow professionally.

Economy, insurgency, social structures as well as lack of human resources have never allowed the region to grow in the media sector as it should have been. It is almost a cottage industry in most of the states where professional approach, working environment and salary packages are completely in nascent stage and cannot be compared to the rest of India.

States like Arunachal Pradesh and Nagaland do not ensure basic freedom of the press and that is evident to some extent in Manipur also, where the media has several run-ins with a number of insurgent groups of the state. In these states, media generally goes for unedited visuals of press conferences, running it full, for fear of getting in trouble with these groups.

In the entire Northeast, except Assam, the television news appears to be mostly passive coverage of events. They cover the news, events and happenings and report in a straight forward way. There is no hidden interpretation and it is straight bland news. The probity angle is completely missing in all the news. The natural instinct of journalists questioning any public issue is absent to.

If there is a landslide or an accident or a bomb blast, it will be reported. But the news will not question why or how it had happened whether that could have been avoided and what were the factors involved.

The television media in the region, except Assam, does not take an analytical route. They do plain reporting, may be due to the complex socio-political situation, where there is always a parallel underground society of the insurgents. Even in Manipur, where the society is very advanced and active, the analytical route is not very visible.

Only in Assam, television media is capable of turning any event into a major social issue. The television media of other states do not have that capability. Unfortunately, that capability of Assam has been misused for the purpose of 'agenda journalism' by the management of all four news channels of the state, thereby bringing in complete anarchy there.

Assam

The media in Assam has a long history of 160 years. But that is predominantly print media. Television is roughly a decade and half old. In fact, it is still in the evolution stage.

Assam's media can be divided into two parts: before 1985 and after. The media before 1985 was more leaning towards literature with just a sprinkling of news. The hard news was never the priority and the journalism was more of service. However, post-1985, it all changed and print medium grew explosively, and professionalism started creeping in.

Today, Guwahati boasts of the highest number of dailies coming out from any city of India. The last count keeps the tally at 18, the majority of them being medium-sized newspapers.

For a region that was habituated to see 15 minutes of evening news bulletin on DD, the new millennium changed all that. As more than two generations of Northeasterners raised on the daily diet of DD news of ribbon-cutting and seminar inauguration by the regional ministers, the year 2003 saw advent of the first private satellite television news channel in the region, after a series of attempts made by the local cable networks to give an alternative perspective through local news bulletins between 2000 and 2003.

Obviously Guwahati was the pioneer as it saw an alternative news perspective, other than that of DD, in their television screens since 4 March 2001, when cable TV operators joined hands to produce local news bulletin through Prag News.

It was a brave attempt with no finance and no technology and for that, television news of the region would always remember Kaushik Nath for attempting such a bulletin. Prag News was widely popular across Guwahati despite its technological inadequacies. The reach of Prag News spread across Brahmaputra valley, which opened the eyes of entrepreneurs about the potential of a private television news channel.

Thus, came The Northeast Television (NETV). NETV started beaming through the satellite from 16 March 2003, and it was an instant hit as the channel could be viewed from anywhere in India. It tried to cover various events of the region and in fact held live broadcast of many big events. This caught the imagination of the Northeast people as they found their regional news 24 hours on screen.

But for the NETV, the biggest challenge was language as there was no common language for the seven Northeastern states. Soon, it started broadcasting in a host of languages in order to cater the demand of various tribes and states.

At one point of time, they were broadcasting in 10 different languages. They were: Hindi, English, Assamese, Nagamese, Garo, Nepali, Bengali, Boro, Manipuri, and Mizo. The NETV was certainly the only channel in the whole of the country, which used to broadcast in so many languages.

With such language challenge in this region, NETV had no other option but to focus on the main bulletin in Assamese and English to remain politically powerful. The rest of the bulletin was mere translations and as per the availability of feed of the targeted area, those were added in other language bulletins.

In a bid to expand horizontally, the NETV handed over the district correspondentship to the most dominating cable operator of that district. This means whoever had the highest number of cable connections of one district became district correspondents. It was a business decision by NETV so that they could be placed in prime bandwidth for easy viewing.

The NETV got popular but in the process a breed of non-journalists (cable operators) across the state were unleashed to cover the news who had no idea of what news or journalism was. That decision permanently changed and affected the quality of journalism in the state. The NETV management was least bothered about quality and ethics, as they only wanted the visual of the story. They initiated a wave of aggressive agenda journalism, which was conceived by Manoranjana Singh, co-owner and the then wife of Matang Singh.

Nevertheless, NETV ruled the sky of the Northeast completely. Being the only private broadcaster, they became the cynosure of all eyes. Despite the fact that NETV was owned by controversial politician Matang Singh through his Positive Television Private Limited, it gained popularity among the people of the region. Matang Singh was a politician from Assam and was a Union minister in the Narasimha Rao ministry, but later was expelled from Congress. He also used his channel to score his political battle with Chief Minister Tarun Gogoi. Despite having a regional profile, the NETV focused on Assam because of obvious logistic reasons and their agenda journalism eventually became a norm in Assam.

The lack of trained manpower also did not help the situation. Television news came all of a sudden to the region and exploded as neither viewers knew what to expect from a local TV channel nor was there adequate manpower in the region to manage the same. It was a free-for-all and total experimentation mode. Unfortunately, this trend still continues.

The NETV however kept their focus on the preparation of National Games, which ultimately took place in January 2007 after several postponements. That was one issue the NETV persistently followed for four years, never giving any room to the government.

Most of the seasoned journalists of the print until then however did not consider television journalism as an alternative career as they treated it with contempt. Television reporters were viewed only as 'Sound Byte Soldiers' rather than as journalists.

As the NETV unleashed power of television journalism in the region, the local cable operators started organising themselves and airing local news from many parts of the region. The local cable channels sprung up in Imphal, Aizwal and Shillong, but everywhere the modus operandi was same. Mostly the content was cinema, live coverage of local events and an evening news bulletin from a makeshift studio.

With no competition around, whatever the NETV did become a benchmark for others to follow in the later years. There was neither any orientation for the journalists nor any serious efforts for content development. Unquestioned fulfilments of political agenda of the management remained the primary goal for all the journalists of NETV, who were expected to work 16-17 hours a day.

A few upstarts of the print media in pursuit of individual growth and power made the situation even more complex as they jumped on the bandwagon with their own show. They flowed with the agenda journalism of NETV for personal materialistic gain.

As the power of television media was realised by all, three groups started planning satellite television channels in Assam. The cable operators floated a company called AM TV bringing together a number of big names, while powerful Congress Minister Dr Himanta Biswa Sarma started his endeavour, and thirdly Mr Sanjib Jaiswal, a complete outsider also applied alone for licenses for a satellite channel.

AM TV could not get the license, but Dr Himanta Biswa Sarma and Mr Sanjib Jaiswal got clearances to broadcast their channels. However, it was Dr Sarma who went on air first with NewsLive through his wife-led company Pride East Entertainment Pvt. Ltd. in January 2008.

NewsLive was headed by one of the few actually trained television journalists—Syed Zarir Hussain, a former Press Trust of India (PTI) correspondent who also had a brief training in British Broadcasting

Corporation (BBC). Along with Atanu Bhuyan, a print journalist, had led the channel far more professionally than NETV. Journalists were trained, given some exposure and there was cohesion amongst the team.

The basic approach and content of the channel was Assam-centric. There was stark difference between the professional approach of NewsLive with better news and technology as compared to that followed by NETV.

On the other hand, NETV by virtue of the name had to maintain the approach of the Northeast with 10 language news. This was not taken well by the city dominated viewers of Assam, and opened up for News Live its first inroads into Assam.

The channel NewsLive took a subtle approach in the beginning and for the first year or so it went on smoothly, and a new benchmark of journalism with professional outlook, approach and content was attempted. That was the reason NewsLive could not only penetrate into NETV's domain but within a very short time, it outsmarted NETV and took the pole position that they have maintained ever since, despite stiff competition from others.

However, both the NewsLive and NETV had one common problem. Both the channels were owned by Congress politicians and must never accepted with open arms by ordinary viewers of Assam, who have been traditionally anti-Congress and anti establishment.

The same year saw addition of the third satellite channel in Assam. The name of the channel was DY365, owned by Mr Sanjib Jaiswal through Brahmaputra Teleproductions Private Ltd. This channel was headed by some known faces of Assamese journalism. Mr Manoj Kumar Goswami was the Editor-in-Chief, Mr Pranay Bardoloi, Managing Editor and Mr Manoram Gogoi, Deputy Editor. The channel was initially in four languages, Assamese, Bengali, Hindi and English. Later, however, both NewsLive and DY365 became Assamese channels.

DY365 immediately struck a chord with the viewers as the ownership was free from political baggage. It was clean news and despite technological disadvantage, it was well accepted by Assamese educated middle class.

The basic content of NewsLive was infotainment, mixing a popular cocktail of cultural shows, entertainment programmes and Assamese cinema along with news bulletins. Their TRPs soared and by 2010 they had established an unassailable lead over the other two channels.

With three TV channels operating out of Guwahati, there were naturally huge competitions and inadequate trained professionals. All eyed screen domination through shrill sound bites and masala news. But all followed the characteristics of infotainment as none of them were really full time 24x7 news channels.

The definition of news was changed by two persons in those years. One was Manoranjana Singh of the NETV and the other was Atanu Bhuyan of NewsLive. Both went on for complete aggressive news with focus on trivial matters, disregarding all ethics, and yet their brand of journalism became the yardstick. However, it was NewsLive that was fast gaining leadership and eventually raced way ahead of NETV as well as DY365.

As the gap between NewsLive and NETV widened, there was management squabble inside NETV, leading the husband and wife duo of Matang Singh and Manoranjana Singh to split. This helped DY365 to take the firm second spot in 2010. Since then, it has been NewsLive on top and DY365 in the second with other television channels coming in the other positions.

Initially, DY 365 tried to remain the torchbearer in value-based journalism but soon got drowned in the battle of TRP as the wisdoms were thrown out of the window to join the rat race and remain relevant with the advertisers.

With news standards of the editorial departments of these channels abysmally low, the situation further deteriorated as the management of the TV channels started pushing their main agenda to become power brokers.

By 2010, the money from Ponzi schemes started flowing in and with that came more television channels. First it was Manoranjana Singh who launched Frontier TV, after losing a public battle to regain NETV from her former husband Matang Singh.

Then on 27 May 2011, Primer TV came into being with another Ponzi scheme operator Chandan Das of Jeevan Surakha fame, becoming the owner. Just before that, News Time was launched by another Ponzi scheme operator, Rose valley. Suddenly Assam had six satellite television channels. Besides the market leader NewsLive and DY365, there were NETV, News Time, Frontier TV and Primer TV.

By 2012, NETV had been reduced to a non-entity as ownership problem raged on and the employees started flocking to other channels. Both Frontier TV and Prime TV began well. Frontier TV was led by veteran Manorajana Singh and Prime TV was led by Manjit Mahanta and Pranjal Phukan. Mahanta was veteran from print media and Pranjal Phukan was with the NETV.

But the whirlpool of the TRPs and sustained success of NewsLive through coverage of trivial issues changed the content of the television channel of Assam forever. Apparently, the briefing given to a field reporter in any TV channel of Assam was to shout as much as possible and get the first visuals.

Contents Piorities

With NewsLive's real owner being Dr Himanta Biswa Sharma, the most influential politician of Assam between 2004-2014, he relentlessly pursued his own political agenda. That heavily influenced the contents of NewsLive.

The DY365 remained firmly in the number two position as it built the entire profile on being anti-Himanta Biswa Sarma. There were hardly any news bulletins, which had no news against Himanta Biswa Sarma. He nurtured his Chief Ministerial aspiration and used his channel to push his career, but the DY365 relentlessly went after him never allowing him a breather. It picked up Akhil Gogoi, a maverick grass root anti-corruption crusader, in their battle against Dr Sarma.

Assam then witnessed a battle between DY365 and NewsLive on two fronts. One was channel rivalry and another was the political rivalry between Dr Himanta Biswa Sarma and Akhil Gogoi, as they became the pivot of Assam politics and television in 2012-2014.

Both the television channels remained glued to and garnered TRPs from these two personalities, as both remained TV audience

are overlooked, but all minor incidents are blown up, even in the case of a simple burglary.

The content of the Assamese TV news may be shallow but one has to admit that it has deep impact. Since 2010, almost all the major social political issues have been governed by the television media and by 2012, the print medium has lost the edge over television, as far as the impact is concerned, despite the fact they are doing far more serious journalism.

Northeast Media Scene in Other States

Impact-wise, the television media scene of other states is not healthy. Except in Mizoram and to some extent Manipur, television journalism has not grown professionally in other states. The size of the population and economics of the state do not allow any satellite channels to grow from any other parts of the region. Manipur has made a brave attempt within their small population, but that is hardly evident in Meghalaya, Tripura, Nagaland, and Arunachal Pradesh.

Here is a brief account of all the states of the region.

Manipur

Free from the TRP race, the cable channels of Manipur still have substance. From the perspective of Hindi and Assamese satellite channels, many will argue that Manipuri channels are stale.

Manipur does not have satellite channels as they cannot afford so, given that the population is too small. Besides, there is the multiple language challenge. The Meithei is the dominant language in the four valley districts but in the surrounding hill districts, it is the Nagamese.

Manipur has three major cable-based television networks. They are ISTV, Impact TV and Image TV. Two of them operate out of Imphal and one operates from Kakching. All of them run three daily news bulletins starting from afternoon 3 pm. But their content is largely coverage of event, interviews and talk shows. The news is straight, without much of commentary.

Their reach is four valley districts and parts of Churachandpur and Chandel. They cover mostly local news, government and private functions, local activities, interview of achievers in any fields, besides covering manmade or natural disasters as well as rallies and protest march. All the channels carry prime time talk shows, but the participation is not aggressive like that of Assam-based or even Hindi channels.

The ISTV is the market leader, while Impact TV is coming up through an equity model, but they are yet to make a major mark on the society. Although Manipur values news, it is difficult to bring in the normal aggressive style of journalism because of major social issues and insurgent groups. So the media houses remain strictly confined to covering the events, remaining careful to not give an an opinion on the same.

Besides these three, there are a few local cable network news channels in Chandel and Churachandpur, and they have evening bulletins with local news.

Meghalaya

The Meghalaya scene is more curious. The state has three distinct zone of Jaintias, Khasis and Gaors, each speaking their own language and hence there is no single state-wide common television channel. Similarly, they too do not have any satellite channels, and a number of local cable networks are present, of which PCN is the widest and oldest cable network.

Besides PCN, there are Ri Khasi, Media Plus, T7, Batesi and Net Vision. Some of the channels are indirectly owned by politicians. The news channel covers political, social and environment issues. Then again they do basic coverage but do not bring in probity, and hence aggression is highly lacking in these channels.

Media plus, Batesi and T7 are aired daily while the rest are aired on Sunday and Net Vision, a Hindi news channel is aired on Saturday.

Television news here is mostly about functions, government and private, and incidents. There is no analysis. In fact, there are very less viewers of local TV news in Meghalaya because no 24-hour channel is present. People largely depend on newspapers.

A very small percentage of journalists are involved in private broadcast media here. There are no big financiers. The owners are mostly regular journalists themselves.

Nagaland

Except two and half hours of programme in local Doordarshan, that includes local news (15 minutes) and regional news bulletins, there is no local private TV channels in Nagaland. Unlike in other places, the viewers in the state prefer cable connections, rather than DTH (direct to home).

The people in general prefer English, Nepali and Korean channel, which are provided by cable operators not DTH services. For example Korean entertainment channels like Arirang and KBC are so popular; the young people at Kohima have formed Arirang Korean viewers' club. The channel also aired a monthly 30 minute programme on Naga music, produced by High Dawn Media, a local production firm, for six months in 2007-08.

Cable operators distribute local entertainment events and programmes organised by the churches of different denominations with deferred live telecast. In most cases they are not edited, recorded versions are aired as it is. In Nagaland, as the television media is not strong, the operators do not take any chance and play the press conference full without edit to avoid the wrath of politicians or any radical groups.

Arunachal Pradesh

The first electronic media started in the month of July, 2000, through Guwahati Doordarshan Kendra (DDK). Journalist Taro Chatung, who was working as stringer for DDK Guwahati used to send news for DD from Itanagar.

In 2001, Taro Chatung started a sponsored news programme in the name of 'News and Views', which lasted for five years. This programme was telecast for 15 minutes every day from 7:15 pm to 7:30 pm through Itanagar DDK.

Chatung, who was an Arunachal Pradesh Civil Service officer, left his government job to be the first man in the state to work in electronic media. His News and Views was so popular in Arunachal Pradesh that people still remember him for his show. It was a unique show in which he himself was the reporter, anchor and producer.

When NETV was launched on 16 March 2003, Chatung joined as a correspondent and worked there until 2010. During this period, many people joined electronic media, but there were no channels as such from the state. Bamang Felix, who is now an MLA and parliamentary Secretary of Intellectual Property Rights (IPR) and Education, was an anchor and produced one weekly TV show named Prime Time in Itanagar DDK between 2002-03.

A hotel owner Arun Mehta started a weekly cable news programme, Arunachal Diary in Vista Vision Cable TV network, Itanagar, for nearly three years. Meanwhile Hiba Kaha, who was associated with Taro Chatung as camera-person in NETV and DD programme, came up with a separate news bulletin called Aaz Ki Aawaz that was telecasted in Itanagar and Naharlagun once in a week.

Later journalist Tumter Riba started another independent news agency called Arunachal News Network, and used to telecast a weekly news programme in Vista Vision Cable network in Itanagar, as well as in Nahalagun Cable TV network.

But it was not regular and later stopped in between 2011-12. In the same way, Hiba Kaha's Aaz Ki Aawaz was also stopped. For more than two years, there was vacuum of television news.

In 2013, Eastern Sky Media started a news service through News Express satellite channel. They bought a half hourly slot from them and are since airing news content daily. The bulletin can be seen in the DTH platform from everywhere.

In the local cable network, the Arunachal TV (ATV) is ruling the roost. But traditionally, Arunachal media has been only covering events.

Apart from these, various cable operators in different places in Arunachal Pradesh are involved in electronic news coverage. Places like Ziro, Aalo, Teju, Tawang, Bomdila, Seppa, Roying, and Anini, have their own news programmes. The style of the news is straight as political twists are not followed by general public, and media also avoid the same.

Mizoram

In Mizoram, there is one cable channel, LPS and a satellite channel, Zonet. Zonet in the market leader and their news is of very high standard, while the LPS is an old warhorse with their production starting way back in 1992.

Zonet cable TV network, now Zonet Cable TV Pvt. Ltd., was established in 2004 by three eminent Mizo journalists namely—K. Sapdanga, the owner, Editor and Publisher of *Vanglaini Daily*, the biggest daily in the state; a popular writer, Vanneihtluanga, Editor and Publisher of *Lengzem Monthly*, the biggest monthly in the state; and R.K. Lianzuala, a former News Editor of All India Radio, Aizawl and the first journalist from Northeast India to selected by the British Council to undergo a training in Broadcast Journalism in the UK and successfully completed the same in 1999.

Zonet was established as a partnership firm and can now claim to be the most successful partnership firm in Mizoram. The network has now successfully completed its 7th year and in terms of viewership and quality, it is generally growing with the people's support.

After being in the profession for seven years, Zonet Cable TV Pvt. Ltd. has now become a fully-licensed Mizo satellite TV channel that provides viewers with a wholesome 24-hour entertainment, films, music, career and family-based content.

Content-wise, Zonet is far ahead than most of the news outlets of the other hilly states and their style of news is also quite aggressive. But it is not a full-time news channel. It is a general entertainment channel, and also carries news and current affairs programmes.

During the past seven years, Zonet has organised three successful seasons of Mizo Idol, a singing competition among the Mizos. Due to its successful ratings, it received a top position among other Mizo general entertainment channels. Currently, the channel is featuring a number of successful shows, such as Look Alike, Strong Man Contest, Red Ribbon State Level Football Tournament, Dancing competition, Science exhibition, Quiz programme, Tiptoppers, Acapella, Mizo Choir Contest (Beat Contest) as well as interviews with successful Mizos in various walks of life and popular leaders. The channel's most popular show, Mizo Idol has been one of the top-ranked shows ever since its launch.

These local TV channels have tremendous impact on the society as politicians and society leaders vie for appearance therein. Both the channels televise the state assembly proceedings live and also counting of votes in the elections, but coverage of Zonet has greater depth.

Tripura

In Tripura, there is one satellite channel, Khobor 365 Din, which is owned by Brand Value, Kolkata. It is operating from Tripura capital, Agartala. The channel is actually owned by Kolkata-based Rose Valley group, which is a Ponzi scheme operator and is the only Bengali television channel in northeast India.

Besides Khobor 365 Din, 20 other cable network based local TV channels have been operating in Tripura, mostly in Agartala. These TV channels are broadcasting a mix bag of current affairs, entertainment and sports news. Content-wise, they are growing as it is a usual mix of news and entertainment.

As far as the impact and content are concerned, the Tripura TV media is quite effective and organised, and in some way they are aggressive too. However, the impact of the TV channels is not massive, but it is increasing by the day.

However like Assam, Tripura also suffers from lack of professional manpower as the knowledge base of anchors, producers, writers and reporters of the state television channels are average and professional acumen is also ordinary. Gradually, however, things are improving.

Conclusion

In terms of technology and final onscreen output, Assam is far ahead than the rest, and is almost at par with any of the regional channels of the India. But content-wise, progressively it is losing ground in terms of quality owing to the TRP race and inadequate trained professionals.

Mizoram and Manipur are not technologically advanced as Assam; but content-wise, although it appears much more bland at

7

SHRAVAN GARG

The Plight of Prime Time

I wonder what we should feel about India's news channels: happy, satisfied, proud? Or totally or partially disappointed! Considering the vast and ever-increasing population and the growing hunger for information from all across the globe, do we have a subscriber-market-revenue space left for more players to participate and invest in electronic media? In reality, the things may be different from television industry's artificial glamour and charm. The definition of news is changing faster than our imagination. With national politics, film & entertainment, crime and sports occupying nearly half of the total prime time of peak hours, i.e., 7 pm to 11 pm of major national news channels, one can understand the plight of other important segments of life requiring equal attention. For example, the news coverage of 'education', which was a meagre 1.10 per cent of total prime time in the year 2005 dropped further to 0.69 per cent in 2013. This is the period in which the field of education took a big leap forward across the nation with India emerging as one of the biggest exporters of talent to developed countries of the world. The natural and an expected fall-out could have been a more comprehensive TV news coverage of education and academics, and greater coverage to the country's educational achievements. But that did not happen. Not surprisingly, the TV news coverage given to health and medicine related issues too was recorded 1.20 per cent of the total prime time in 2005 and it dropped further to 1.06 per cent in 2013. We know for certain how much money and concern has been invested by the country in increasing the life span of every single Indian and what kind of expansion has taken place in the area of health and medical sciences. Science and technology is one field in which India is out to compete with the rest of the world, but TV news media seems to have a limited interest in even this important field; and its prime time coverage dropped from 1.53 in 2008 to 0.55 in 2013. As for agriculture related coverage, well, it was already very low at 0.10 per cent in 2005 and slumped further down to 0.05 in 2013. The entire world knows the great story of India's successful Green Revolution.

Little wonder that all major TV news channels are competing with each other in almost same areas of interest and with generally identical contents on the strengths of their exclusivity in visuals, graphics and anchoring. No denying the fact that TV news content has become largely market-driven, and market forces are controlling the flow of advertisement revenue. Films & entertainment is fast replacing serious content. National politics (11.60%), sports (10.70%), crime (9.40%) and international affairs (8.60) used to occupy the top four coverage slots during prime time of six national news channels in 2005 with film & entertainment getting only 6.10 per cent and that too after state politics (7.10%), legal (6.90%) and business industry (6.30%). But today film & entertainment is among the top three, i.e., third after national politics and sports. Reasons are not difficult to understand. Politics has become the bread for TV news channels, and sports and entertainment the cheese and the butter.

News broadcasting business is estimated at over ₹20 billion today and is witnessing a multifold increase. As of January 2015, India had 405 news and current affairs channels compared to 425 for entertainment. Compare this with the situation when we had just one TV channel and it used to provide everything—from news to entertainment to agriculture to sports.

What could be the reason for this phenomenal rise in the number of channels? Should it be attributed to the globalisation of our economy! Could the reasons be attributed to the growing corruption in national/regional politics and the subsequent generation of black money? These questions can lead us into the details of media ownership patterns. It is being alleged that 'unnamed' politicians, big corporates, business houses, builders and some 'faceless investors' are also behind the investment in electronic media. In fact, it is not only the TV channels, but the entire media that is witnessing a big change. The Indian media industry is expected to grow rapidly at 18.4

per cent with a size of ₹918 billion (PWC India, Entertainment and Media Outlook 2013).

But how does one then deal, analyse or explain the issue of trivialisation of content in such an investment-friendly and growth-oriented industry?

Trivialisation of content in TV news channels is allegedly becoming rampant and no one questions the inherent reportage or its packaging. Viewers or consumers have little or no say. They have an option to surf and switch over to another channel but the story is almost the same at each stop. There is no escape. Content is being presented in a well-organised sellable package and the TV anchors in their colourful dresses and make-up generally appear 'emotionless'.

With regional politics, regional aspirations, and regional demands increasingly dominating national politics and Hindi occupying an important positions at all levels of communication, Hindi media, particularly Hindi channels, are penetrating new areas of viewership. This is leading to increased competition among TV news channels to garner a larger chunk of revenue and viewership. As Rajdeep Sardesai puts it:

> Hindi news channels are faced with a credibility crisis. The credibility depends on the systems and checks that you have in place to see that citizen journalism doesn't just become a gimmick—occasionally it works beautifully—like the autistic child whose father caught on camera the boy being denied entry into a plane, saying that would be dangerous for fellow travellers. That is the ideal kind of citizen journalism.

Dr N. Bhaskar Rao, Chairman of the Centre for Media Studies (CMS) describing the flip side says: "There are accusations of arrogance, insensitivity, bias, inaccuracies, sensationalism, stereotypes, trivialisation, conflict of interest and disappearing lines between news and views."[1] When Justice Markandeya Katju, immediately after taking over as Chairman of the Press Council of India (PCI) in 2011, raised the issue of trivialisation of news,

1. *http://www.academia.edu/8164652/Jaggi_Ruchi_2009_._Popularity_vs._Credibility_An_analysis_of_public_perception_of_sensationalism_in_Indian_television_news._Manthan._Vol._4_Issue_December_ISSN_0974-7141*

particularly on TV channels, there erupted a huge debate on the role of media. Justice Katju's concern was that the media, especially TV channels, were making a fuss of trivial issues not concerning the daily life of large masses. He commented:

> Hundreds of reporters and photographers are deputed for the coverage of a fashion show while very few would take care to pay attention to say, the suicide of farmers or the issues concerning people living below poverty line.

He, therefore, strongly advocates constituting a Media Council replacing the Press Council and bringing electronic media too under its purview along with print. Electronic channels did not offer any support to Katju's proposal on the plea that they have their own body to monitor the content.[2] It is being repeatedly said that cricket, crime and cinema largely dominate TV news. Of the total prime time on six national channels—crime, cinema (films & entertainment) and cricket (sports) consumed about 28 per cent of all the story topics in 2013.

The issue of trivialisation of news at the expense of credibility is also related to the cost of generating content. Compared to print media, the cost of generating news content independently for electronic medium is expensive. Many channels can ill-afford it. Coupled with this is the ever-increasing distribution cost and comparatively low generation of revenue. It is, therefore, not surprising that even national news TV channels focus more on local events. The whole media went overboard in its coverage when following his illness, Amitabh Bachchan was admitted for treatment in a hospital in 2005. Thus, between November 28 and December 28 2005, private news channels devoted more than 700 minutes of their prime time coverage to the illness of a Bollywood megastar. Top Hindi channels devoted a whopping 166 minutes of prime time on November 30 itself, the day Amitabh Bachchan was operated upon. Channels could afford to put all of their resources at a single point as it was close to their production centres. An analysis of the news content during prime time may lead to a conclusion that not only

2. *http://m.thehindu.com/news/national/article2629257.ece/?page=6*

national politics, sports (cricket), film, entertainment (cinema) and crime dominate the prime time coverage, the coverage of events is generally centred around the national capital, Mumbai and few other metropolitan cities. When a 14-month-old boy, Krishna, accidentally falls into an empty 100 feet deep borewell, in a remote Chhatarpur district of Madhya Pradesh in December 2014 and ends up losing his life, it does not stir national news channels to the same fever pitch as compared to the phenomenal coverage given to a boy called Prince from Haryana, in July 2006. When Prince, a six-year old, fell into a 60-feet deep borewell, almost all the national television channels deployed their resources in the coverage of the rescue operation. It was a Friday evening of July 2006 when Prince fell into the borewell and was saved also by Monday morning. During the 50 hours period, one Hindi channel which covered the operation live was watched by more than 40 per cent of Hindi language news viewers, while the share of the other prominent Hindi channels over the same period languished in single digits. National TV news channels could afford to press their cameras and manpower in Haryana, which is in the vicinity of the National Capital Region (NCR), but there were few takers for Chhatarpur as the input cost would have been much higher compared to the gains in terms of the TRP (television rating point). Cost-effectiveness is always preferred when it comes to coverage of an event or happening, irrespective of its human interest value or importance. Moreover, most broadcasters lack resources and even patience to send teams on assignment to remote parts of country. Most media platforms operate for money and power, and TV news broadcasters are no exception. "The higher a programme's television rating points are, the more money a broadcaster can demand from advertisers for airtime during that show. As a result, many broadcasters try to shape their programming to deliver the highest ratings. Advertisers in turn, wield considerable influence over the sorts of shows that broadcasters produce," says Krishna Kaushik. "Nothing astonishing, therefore, that the 'Prince' of Haldehri village of Haryana's Kurukshetra district, not far from Delhi, got TV news channels better ratings than even the Mumbai train bombings of 11 July 2006, in which over 200 people were killed".

India, and thank God for it) as manufacturing content. That's because real stories are becoming difficult to do, or atleast to sell", Kaveree Bamzai had commented way back in 2005[8] and the scene may not have much changed even after over nine years.

Rajdeep Sardesai said in December 2014: "People today watch TV as if they were enjoying some kind of a 'Nautanki'. And we cannot stop this by making a noise only. We are not making some film like Chennai Express or Ek Tha Tiger. It's purely a news programme."[9]

Take a note of this reality also: It suits people with power and/or money at all places—be they politicians, bureaucrats, money-lenders, contractors or all sorts of vested interest groups—that TV watching population is fed more with or addicted to masala entertainment and reality shows rather than the news depicting country's actual reality. Then people don't ask questions about the successes and failures of welfare programmes, non-fulfilment of promises made in the poll manifestoes. Viewers' focus gets easily shifted on the popularity and successes of TV serials, designer clothes, Star Wars, birthday parties and celebrations. Suicides of farmers or corruption in welfare schemes or collapse of a bridge leading to deaths of poor labourers at some district place would not find as much space in TV News coverage as some *dharna* at Jantar Mantar in Delhi or information about cancellation/delay of flights due to fog. TV news is conceived and anchored on the consideration of attracting greater TRPs, and it is generally projected that majority of viewers are not interested in issues relating to farmers and tribals or developmental activities. May be because of this belief that when thousands of tribals from parts of Madhya Pradesh and Chhattisgarh staged a foot march from Gwalior to Delhi demanding protection to their rights on what they called, "Jal, Jangal, Jamin", were not given the kind of attention or coverage they rightfully deserved.

"TV covers everything from a funeral to a Friday cricket match with the same sense of breathless urgency. If everything is important

8. *http://indiatoday.intoday.in/story/tabloidization-of-media-and-news-channels-in-india/1/193902.html*

9. *http://www.exchange4media.com/Dialogue/InterView.aspx?ID=685*

and nothing is trivial, than what is news," asks sociologist Shiv Visvanathan.[10] The problem, in fact, lies in finding out what would actually sell and how. No one really knows about it. The channel heads would, on the other hand, keep arguing that trivial TV is the exception and not the rule, and points to a larger crisis of content that all media faces.

And lastly, should Indian news channels be made to share the charge of trivialisation?

It was in 1982, when during my three-month stay in London for a media course from April to June, I was in the midst of a number of events taking place at the same time. Britain was at war with Argentina over the issue of Falklands, football World Cup was taking place, and so was Wimbeldon. A Pope was visiting for the first time too. But what was the British media mostly engaged with? Princess Diana's pregnancy. She was giving birth to her first child. The details of the hospital distance from the palace, how much time it would take to reach there, who would be her doctor, and so on. Everything else while occupying media space was behind the coverage afforded to Diana's pregnancy. That was in 1982, but what is different today? Now it is the Duchess of Cambridge Kate Middleton's exquisite outfits, her public appearances, her pregnancy and child birth, which continue to occupy prime time media space.

Things are surely changing in TV news from what they were earlier, like when in 2006 Sandeep Unnithan had sarcastically commented: "TV reporters from the '*Aap ko kaisa lagta hai* (how do you feel)' school of journalism routinely quiz their subjects with this line. When asked how he felt when his older brother Shammi was in the ICU, actor Shashi Kapoor retorted that he felt like dancing."[11] But much remains to be addressed and accomplished. This will happen only when the wisdom of real viewers would prevail and the difference between news and trivia is publicly discussed and highlighted. We are surely witnessing an explosive growth of Indian media phenomenon

10. *http://indiatoday.intoday.in/story/indian-tv-channels-redefine-news-to-cater-to-new-viewing-preferences/1/180088.html*

11. *http://indiatoday.intoday.in/story/indian-tv-channels-redefine-news-to-cater-to-new-viewing-preferences/1/180088.html*

in general and TV news channels in particular, and this growth is enjoying support from the economy.

References

Ahmad, Irfan (2015). "Gauging The Language", *The Hindu*. 16 February.

Bamzai, Kaveree (2015). "Of Tabloidization of News Channels in India: INDIASCOPE", *India Today. Indiatoday.intoday.in*. 16 February.

Exchange4media.com (2015). "Welcome to Exchange4media: The Media For Media". 16 February.

Jaggi, Ruchi (2009). "Popularity Vs. Credibility: An Analysis of Public Perception of Sensationalism in Indian Television News", *Manthan*. 4, (December). 16 February.

Sabherwal, Simran (2015). "Broadcast Industry Has Reached A Plateau: Uday Shankar". *Exchange4 media.mobi*. 16 February.

Sardesai, Rajdeep (2015). "Rajdeep Sardesai,Consulting Editor,India Today Group". *Exchange4media.com*. 16 February.

The Hindu (2015). "Justice Markandey Katju Clarifies", *The Hindu*, 16 February.

Unnithan, Sandeep (2015). "Sensationalism: 24-Hour TV Channels Redefine News to Cater to New Viewing Preferences: Cover Story". *India Today. Indiatoday.intoday.in*. 16 February..

8

SONIA SINGH

News *versus* Talk

Has Talk Replaced Journalism?

Talk is cheap! An old idiom now reinterpreted to redefine television channel programming and TV journalism not just in India but the world. In the last five years, the most startling new trend emerging in television news in India, is talk, talk and more talk.

Take a look at this breakup of what's on our screens every night at prime time done by the Media Lab at the Centre for Media Studies (CMS). Except for Doordarshan (DD) and surprisingly the Hindi channel ABP news, the breakup of air time is overwhelmingly dominated by debate. (Times Now has not been monitored by CMS in Table 8.1)

News *versus* Talk: The Indian Story

Have we run out of news stories, is on the ground reportage no longer relevant from the different states in a country as large as India? Not at all. To borrow a cliché from Bollywood, at the moment, talk is a formula that seems to be working at least if we go by our controversial TRP (television rating point) system (for the record, NDTV has challenged the veracity of these ratings). Editorial feedback however does tell us that debates seem to be more compelling for viewers, they have a greater 'sticky' factor, a word used in TV terminology to see how long a viewer stays on a given programme. One reason could be that news in its traditional format is being accessed by more and more people as it happens, online or on their phones. So, at the end of the day, at the traditional TV prime time slots, these 'informed viewers' want News Plus i.e., a short update on the big story and then different perspectives of key newsmakers. If increasingly, this has become a gladiatorial contest with the winner often the one with strongest lungs, so much the better for TRPs.

Table 8.1

New versus Special Trends (January-March 2014)

	Aaj Tak	*DD News*	*ABP News*	*Zee News*	*CNN IBN*	*NDTV 24x7*	*Total*
January: % of News Time							
A-News	14.93	50.12	47.95	30.88	22.95	17.96	30.30
B-Special	85.07	49.88	52.05	69.12	77.05	82.04	69.70
Total	100.00	100.00	100.00	100.00	100.00	100.00	100.00
February: % of News Time							
A-News	20.89	46.13	46.55	29.19	21.88	17.49	30.00
B-Special	79.11	53.87	53.45	70.81	78.12	82.51	70.00
Total	100.00	100.00	100.00	100.00	100.00	100.00	100.00
March: % of News Time							
A-News	21.59	44.50	33.64	34.02	24.86	20.17	30.11
B- Special	78.41	55.50	66.36	65.98	75.14	79.83	69.89
Total	100.00	100.00	100.00	100.00	100.00	100.00	100.00

Notes: 1. A-News: It includes news stories
2. B- Special: It includes discussion, debates, features, etc
3. Figures are based on prime time (7-11 pm) coverage of news channels
4. Figures are % of News Time
5. News Time = Prime Time – Advertisement Time

At NDTV, we have also found that a strong story followed by a debate actually adds to the impact of the original story. For instance, our reporter Sonal Mehrotra did an undercover investigation on medical corruption. We found that when we debated this story with experts in the field on our 8 pm debate show, "Left, Right and Centre", the feedback on this story increased greatly. However, this combination of solid journalism followed by reasoned debate is rare; what is becoming the norm is sharply polarised political debate often sparked by little more than a rude comment.

Global Trends: United States and United Kingdom

The United States (US) began this trend in a sense with the Fox news model which was quickly adopted by MSNBC. CNN joined this later and has struggled to catch up. This trend in the US has spread beyond evening viewing to dominate the 24/7 news cycle. I quote some key findings by the Pew Research Centre which establish this.

> The Pew Research Center conducted a special study in 2013 for that year's edition of the State of the News Media in the United States that analyzed changes in the structure and makeup of television news. Following are the highlights of that report.
>
> *Cable*: The format of daytime cable news has evolved over the last five years to look more like prime-time talk programming. Interview segments are now as prominent in daytime cable as they are in prime time. Coverage of live events and live reports dropped in daytime programming by about one-third—from 33 per cent of the newshole in 2007 to 23 per cent in 2012. And the airtime devoted to interviews—which can cost far less to produce–rose from 39 per cent to 51 per cent, equaling the percentage of airtime they fill on cable at night, when partisan talk and debate drive the programming.
>
> A separate analysis of cable in late 2012 finds that, over all, commentary and opinion are far more prevalent on the air (63% of the airtime) than straight news reporting (37%). CNN is the only channel to offer more reporting (54%) than opinion (46%), though by a small margin. By far the highest percentage of opinion and commentary is on MSNBC (85% to 15% reporting). Fox was in between at 55 per cent commentary and 45 per cent reporting.
>
> Over the years, the three main cable news channels have evolved to become much more similar in programming structure. That marks a major change from 2007 when CNN was distinguished by its emphasis on edited packages and MSNBC spent far more time on interviews than either of its rivals. This convergence occurred after major shifts at all three networks. MSNBC changed its formatting most in prime time, Fox in daytime and CNN changed sharply in both day parts.

Interestingly, the United Kingdom (UK) has remained much more conservative in its news broadcasts and even its debates. Indian debate shows have of course produced a whole new breed of 'Shouting Indians' who now dominate the airwaves.

News *versus* Talk: Impact on Budgets

What however are the pros and cons of this news model? The best part from a television management's point of view is that this is much cheaper than traditional news gathering. As advertisement revenues shrink across the board, newsrooms have had to budget carefully. Talk for an hour adds up to content that is quarter the cost of sending television reporters and camera crews across India. Unlike a licensing model, TV revenue in India is largely limited to advertisement, which means constant pressure on budgets.

So if it comes to the bottomline, talk shows may seem like a win-win situation for all concerned, anchors, management, the viewers and of course, the chosen ones, guests who become 'mini celebrities' overnight...often for doing little more than showing up and nodding sagely, some getting just a sentence or two in over the span of a 40-minute debate.

Delhi Domination of News

With most national news channels headquartered in Delhi or Mumbai, views and opinions are often limited to guests from these cities or state capitals where bureaus have the equipment to go live. This then leads to a further narrowing of horizons so that these are the voices that are heard the most often. This is something that editorial management in channels must be aware of and ensure a fair representation of different perspectives. We need to be extremely wary of this urban dominance in our news coverage as well. When we debate why a rape in New Delhi has non-stop coverage as opposed to say a rape in Bundelkhand, it's often a simple matter of logistics. By the time a reporter, camera crew and OB van travel to a remote area, it can be more than 24 hours; by which time, the attention span of a 24/7 viewer has often shifted not to mention the cost involved.

There is of course another more worrying factor, the rape of a woman in urban India invariably attracts more attention than a rape in the Other India. This is a constant battle editors face in a newsroom—how to make viewers care about issues that may not directly impact their lives. The example of the news coverage of an issue like MNREGA is a case in point. Debated in English language studios, the overwhelming view is that this a subsidy India cannot afford. Interestingly, however when you include politicians or activists from the rural heartland, the perspective changes completely. They point to the fact that there is a skewed balance when it comes to reporting subsides for corporates and for the poor. Again, issues like malnutrition or deaths of newborns, which affect thousands of poor children do not get the coverage on prime time as there would be, for example, on the death of one school child in Mumbai or Delhi. The fact that these issues aren't on the political agenda only pushes them further down the news agenda, sadly.

Yet, this can change with concerted effort. As Maharashtra faced its worst drought in years, our Bureau Chief Tejas Mehta travelled to affected areas of Vidarbha. Daily live reports with local voices on the OB, instead of city based commentators, brought the issue live into city drawing rooms, crucial for better understanding of the tragic phenomenon of farmers suicides.

In this context, Table 8.2 of the origin of different news stories is fascinating. It shows that news from Delhi accounts for nearly half of the entire news cycle, other state capitals accounts for just over 10 per

Table 8.2

Story Origin Trends 2008-2013

Story Origin	*% of Prime Time News*					
	2008	*2009*	*2010*	*2011*	*2012*	*2013*
Chennai	1.15	0.57	0.41	1.10	0.51	0.75
Delhi	33.13	38.31	43.18	47.51	48.88	47.24
International	18.55	20.46	13.60	13.82	12.25	7.80
Kolkata	0.98	0.56	1.09	1.41	1.27	1.15
Mumbai	17.50	15.39	16.70	11.77	9.61	8.37
Other State Capitals	7.51	6.81	8.13	8.61	9.13	10.07
Other Towns and Cities	20.93	17.45	16.08	14.72	17.84	23.89
Rural	0.24	0.45	0.80	1.05	0.52	0.72
Total	100.00	100.00	100.00	100.00	100.00	100.00

Notes: 1. Figures are based on prime time (7-11 pm) coverage of 6 national news channels.

2. News channels–Aaj Tak, DD News, NDTV 24x7, CNN IBN, Star News/ABP News and Zee News

cent while rural India is less than 1 per cent. India lives in its villages, was remarked by Mahatma Gandhi; but that is clearly not the case for Indian television. These figures alone should be a wakeup call to all of us.

Conclusion

Indian television journalism is still relatively young but we now need to use the wisdom of our years. What is urgently needed is all-India coverage, both in the context of reporting plus debate. Just talk cannot be the way forward for broadcasters. As someone who's been in the business for over 20 years, I feel strongly the current trend is largely damaging for journalism. My view however isn't as simplistic as talk is bad, not at all. Intelligent debate centred around a serious news story is crucial and can be a great way to cover a news development with a 360-degree perspective. The problem is serious journalism has got lost in this talk fest. Too often the issue being discussed is trivial beyond belief, an whole hour can be devoted to a tweet for instance. Dumbing down of television is a dangerous trend in the misguided belief that this is what viewers want.

In the final analysis, is it Journalism *versus* Talk? It doesn't have to be. Informed talk or debate and dialogue are a crucial aspect to expand a viewer's understanding of a subject. What all of us as television editors have to guard against is confusing shouting matches for debate. Journalism in the public interest is not about catering to the lowest common denominator but informing, illuminating and in some cases educating the viewer. True journalism after all doesn't need to be shouted out to be heard.

9

N.K. SINGH

Half-Truth, Truth and Public Opinion

Studio Discussions: A Great Public Sphere that Lack Impartiality

In his famous book *The Idea of Justice*, Nobel laureate Amatrtya Sen poses a question to the readers,

> There are three children—Anne, Bob and Carla who are quarrelling to get a flute. Anne claims the flute on the ground that she is the only one of three who knows how to play it (the others do not deny this), and that would be quite unjust to deny the flute to the only one who can actually play it. If that is all you knew, the case for giving the flute to the first child would be strong.
>
> But in an alternative scenario, it is Bob who speaks up, and defends his case for having the flute by pointing out that he is the only one among the three who is so poor that he has no toys of his own. The flute would give him something to play with (the other two concede that they are richer and well supplied with engaging amenities). If you had heard only Bob and none of the others, the case for giving it to him would be strong.

The writer presents a third alternative scenario.

> It is Carla who speaks up and points out that she has been working diligently for many months to make the flute with her own labor (the others confirm this), and just when she has finished her work, she complains "these expropriators came along to try to grab the flute away from me" If Carla's statement is all that you heard, you might be inclined to give the flute to her in recognition of her understandable claim t something she has made herself.

Having heard all three and their different lines of reasoning, there is a difficult decision that you have to make. The Utilitarian theorists would justify Anne's claim, the Economic egalitarians would vouch for Bob, while Carla would get immediate favour from Libertarian.

Like in the above scenario, in Ayodhya case too, while the Hindus claimed the place was birth place of Lord Ram and the Muslims do not deny it, the latter claim they are in 'reverse possession' of the land and are owner of it and Hindus do not denying it.

Now the process of arriving at a judicial decision across the world is not a mechanical process. Had it been so, and more so in the era of computerisation, variables could have been quantified and just by the click of a button, decisions could have been made even by a computer operator. Human beings in black robes could have long been done away with.

Judges while making decisions have to take into account such factors that cannot be quantified. They have also to consider the reality that even facts (variables) are time-, space- and situation-subjective.

Studio Discussions and the Role of Anchor-Editor

In a freewheeling seminar-cum-question-answer session, organised by a media house a few months back, two noted firebrand editors-anchors—one from an English channel and another from a Hindi channel—justified their strong opinion-effervescing voyage into their regular evening studio discussions, saying they did have the right to hold an opinion and without opinion, of course, laced with facts the great cause of journalism could not be served.

Truth (loosely mentioned as fact) is nothing but perception built on the basis of past knowledge and present observations obtained through sense organs. In epistemology, therefore, truth, as we know about it, is neither absolute nor pure because capabilities of sense organs vary from man to man. Your truth may not be same as mine.

Both these editors-anchors had had their specs on. Had they removed their spectacles [biases], the composition and quality of audience being addressed would have got blurred, suggesting that their truth (fact) would have changed in a moment. This also suggests that their truth is not the same as it was when they had removed their spectacles [biases]. *Sarp-rajju bhram* (snake-rope illusion) of *advaita Vedanta* more than establishes it. Same rope can look like snake if light conditions are changed. More so when you have a prior knowledge that two days ago a snake was spotted in the hall. *Brahm satyam jagat mithya*—the basic theory of Shankar's *Mayawaad,* which was fully endorsed by Western philosophers including Bradley, hinges on this logic. One of its derivation is that there is no truth that a human being can discern with certainty.

Now to the core issue. The two editors-anchors claimed that in their discussions, they tried to ferret out facts before forming opinion. How many 'facts' and under what trying circumstances? Now suppose they have got certain facts about the beheading of two Indian soldiers ostensibly on Indo-Pak border in Kashmir. Within a few hours, they arrive at an opinion after collecting 'all facts'. And they concluded that it was 'dastardly act' by Pakistani soldiers. Their gesture and utterances in the studios clearly show a sense of outrage and they wanted the "Indian Government to respond in matching terms." Obviously, their arguments also evoke as much drawing-room outrage across the country.

There doubts obviously emerge out of their opinion-cum-fervour for "teach-Pak-a-lesson". Either they have lacked in informing all facts to the viewers or have selectively ignored them or did not know about them. The question is whether they informed the viewers of geo-strategic, geo-diplomatic, Sino-Pak and Indo-China situation, India's strength and vulnerability, rogue character of the rogue state, and its nuclear arsenal *vis-à-vis* India's. 'Just-teach-a-lesson-once- and-for-all' zeal carries attendant problems of loss of innumerable human lives, putting a halt to development and throwing the nation into a vortex of an unintended crisis. Did they tell the masses or in their name to the Government of the day that there could be other quiet but equally powerful ways of hamstringing a brat, Pakistan? Just an outrage in line with general public mood (of a section only which reacts on anything from rape to ramp to rubrics) will not help serve higher levels of journalistic cause.

Even if this section is in majority, it is not 'the Nation'. If a referendum is sought on whether Ram Mandir should be built on a disputed site, they will have a majority in its favour, but this cannot be dubbed as the desire of 'the nation'. A democratic nation is formed of majority opinion plus recognition of minority rights, Constitutional government and government by discussion.

There is another logical fallacy. When somebody feels weak in his argument and he needs to buttress his 'opinion' (or fact?), he takes recourse to 'aptvachan' i.e., quote a verse from the Gita or other credible scripture or a saying of some great men. Here when these two editors-anchors in question say "the nation wants to know" the fact, they actually can be accused of committing two 'wrongs', one, that they never undertook any referendum on the issue and two, that even if the majority wants India to 'teach a lesson', it is not justified in the same way in which a *mandir* on the site is not justified merely on the basis of numerical strength.

Taking up major issues is good effort, a great contribution. Raising the issue of beheading of Indian soldiers on a high pitch is a national cause, even according to their own admission. Common citizens also feel the same. But suppose a month later another "fact" comes to them to the effect that it was a handiwork of some Kashmir terrorists who wanted to create a rift between the two countries or that it was the job of some criminals-smugglers crossing over to the other country and who, first tried to bribe the two soldiers but when the latter did not fall for it, they were killed in that manner by the former.

Will it not cause a blot on an otherwise respectful institution of Editor? What answer will be preferred by an opinioned (if not opinionated as distinguished by one of the two editors) editors to the nation for which they claimed to have dished out their initial opinion (truth)?

There is another logical fallacy in their stock argument, which is known as selective appropriation of facts. Your viewers do not know with what perseverance and resources (both are limited and subjective) they have obtained all facts.

The third argument against editors-anchors lurching towards this or that side under, what they termed as opinion, is that the institution of editors enjoys certain amount of credibility for being impartial. An editor of *People's Daily* or of *Saamanaa* or *Panchjany* has same freedom of expression that these two editors-anchors (who and whose channels are expected to have remained impartial) have. But there is a difference between how viewers attach credibility to the former on one hand and the latter, on the other.

Technically speaking, our (media's) job is to create a marketplace for competing ideas. We should present all facts with perspective without appearing to be glued to one or the other side (of facts). More so in case of studio discussions. Unlike newspaper editorial columns where it is one-way opinion followed by readers comment, studio discussions have a mechanism where discourse is guided by the moderator or anchor (in present case, Editors). Since its character is instant, interactive and informative, the role of moderator shrinks to that of guide rather than a participant.

Now take a recent case in Badaun. Two sisters belonging to a most backward caste (MBC) were found hanging from a tree. Entire media ran non-stop stories, followed by discussions accusing some Yadavs of the village as the culprits. The heat was so intense in the studios that the Uttar Pradesh (UP) government and its Chief Minister were forced to arrest the accused. Later when the Central Bureau of Investigation (CBI) investigated, it was found that the two sisters had hanged themselves out of shame for being in a compromising state with one of the Yadav accused. The CBI recommended closure of the case. The upbeat Chief Minister asked the media if they would apologise for creating wrong perception in the minds of the people of the country.

But hold on. It is not the end of the story. Some journalists from western countries went to cover the story two weeks ago. They sought to re-enact the scene of hanging. They gathered some girls of the same village and urged them to scale the particular branch of the tree from which the two sisters were found hanging. Not a single could reach the branch. So the suicide theory of the CBI proved wrong again. Not to say media again stood vindicated.

Another case is that of Meerut. A few years ago, a rape-cum-murder incident occurred. The media reports pointed fingers at the two accused on the basis of available facts. The trial court convicted the accused by awarding life imprisonment. The accused approached the High court; the latter berated the trial court and acquitted the accused. The state went in appeal to the Supreme Court. The apex court found the High court judgment faulty and endorsed conviction awarded by the trial court. This shows 'truth' is dependent on the capacity of whether the accused or the State in going higher up the judicial ladder. If the state had not approached the apex court, it was media which could have been blamed for wrong reporting. Who is to be faulted in this case?

The danger in expressing opinion as editor-anchor, therefore, is: a) if opinion went wrong subsequently on fact-count, it will cause immense damage to the credibility of the institution, and b) people will remain deprived of a considered and balanced view that can help shape their own perception.

Section V

Issues

10

SUDHIR RINTEN

Entertainment as News Media Content

Coverage of entertainment news is very high in India. Prime time trends of past nine years show that entertainment carries a very prompt position with an average of 11.04 per cent coverage in overall prime time coverage.

Figure 10.1

Trends in Entertainment Coverage in TV News

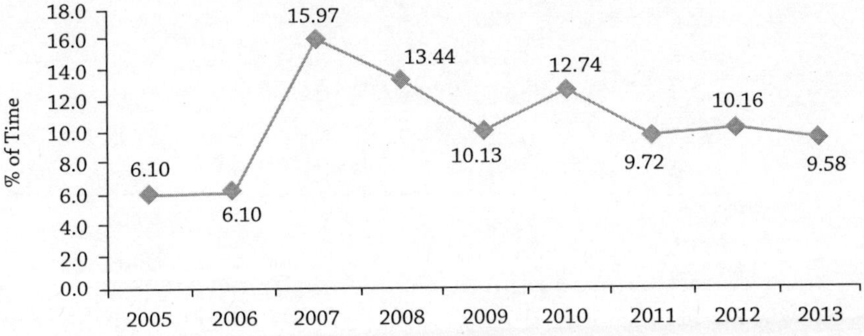

Source: CMS Media Lab.

According to CMS Media Lab reports, coverage of different news broadcasters between 2005-2013 in prime time comprised a large chunk of entertainment news. The average percentage of the different channels in regards to prime time coverage given to entertainment news is as follows: Aaj Tak (17.27%), Zee News (8.89%), Star News (17.73%) and Sahara Samay (7.75%).

One can say that in contrary to popular perception, this trend was not only reflected by Hindi news broadcasters, but also by English news broadcasters. The average of English news channels like CNN IBN and NDTV 24x7 was 15.90 per cent and 8.23 per cent, respectively, between the years 2008-2013. The year 2007 seems to have witnessed high levels of entertainment coverage during prime time cutting across news channels. ABP News (formerly known Star News) topped the chart with 32.03 per cent coverage of entertainment during prime time. Aaj Tak came in second with 23.43 per cent coverage.

Table 10.1

Entertainment Coverage (in % of Time) in Prime Time TV News

Year/News Broadcaster	*Aaj Tak*	*Sahara Samay*	*Star News*	*Zee News*	*NDTV India*	*DD News*	*CNN IBN*	*NDTV 24X7*
2005	7.10	5.50	8.80	4.50	6.70	4.60	NA	NA
2006	15.10	6.80	20.80	15.60	9.90	4.80	NA	NA
2007	23.43	10.95	32.03	18.15	12.51	5.39	NA	NA
2008	24.36	NA	25.79	10.61	NA	2.14	13.50	8.69
2009	20.54	NA	12.42	6.61	NA	1.94	13.65	7.84
2010	22.82	NA	26.98	5.41	NA	3.19	14.77	5.78
2011	14.76	NA	10.90	2.87	NA	3.45	17.70	9.65
2012	16.34	NA	10.10	4.73	NA	2.06	19.95	10.15
2013	10.99	NA	11.75	11.51	NA	2.11	15.85	7.29

Source: CMS Media Lab.

Apart from this prime time coverage, many news channels have their own entertainment shows, which are broadcasted in different time slots. Programmes like Scandal (Aaj Tak, every Saturday at 20:00), Movie Masala (Aaj Tak at 17:30), Love Story (ABP News), Chugali Chachi, Sas Bahu aur Sajish (ABP News), Raat Baaki (NDTV), Night out (NDTV India), Bole Toh Bollywood, Mian, Biwi Aur TV, House arrest and Zee Multiplex (Zee TV), Saas Bahu Aur Betiyaan, Khabar Filmy Hai, and Sshhh (STAR) are some examples of the same. The presence of such shows necessitated the need for an entertainment editor whose task was to requisite entertainment news coverage.

Indian news channels often reflect their voyeuristic face in coverage of different stories of entertainment and crime. The voyeurism is evident and reinforced repeatedly to spur viewership. This approach indeed affects viewership of the programme in an assertive manner. Coverage of the lives of celebrities, their affairs, fights, tours, etc., gives immense pleasure to the contemporary television audience. Audiences are willing to peep into the lives and secrets of their celebrities on television. This satisfies the hunger of voyeurism and fandom.

While satisfying the hunger of voyeurism and fandom to the audiences, channels are presenting programmes like Love Story (ABP News) that provides very personal information like affairs, gossips and visits made at different places; the gossips are being covered to saturate voyeurism. Programmes like this affect news value at a large. This may be considered as unethical but it affects viewership in a very positive manner much to the delight of media organisations.

It is the duty of media to keep the citizenry informed of the state of governance, which mostly puts it at odds with the establishment. A media that is meant to expose the lapses in government and in public life cannot obviously be regulated by the government—it would lack credibility. It is a fundamental paradigm of freedom of speech that media must be free from governmental control in the matter of 'content'—censorship and free speech are sworn enemies. It therefore falls upon the journalist's profession to evolve institutional checks and safeguards, specific to the electronic media that can define the path that would conform to the highest standards of rectitude and journalistic ethics, and guide the media in the discharge of its solemn constitutional duty. News Broadcasters Association (NBA) code of ethics and broadcasting standards)

Broadcasters shall, in particular, ensure that they do not select news for the purpose of either promoting or hindering either side of any controversial public issue. News shall not be selected or designed to promote any particular belief, opinion or desires of any interest group (fundamental principles 5 NBA code of ethics and broadcasting standards), but the broadcasters are promoting films on their platforms due to pressure created by advertisers and producers. Nowadays PR (public relations) agencies have been a very good source for easy and fast flowing content.

Former Press Council of India (PCI) Chairman Retd Justice Markandey Katju was highly critical of the coverage provided to entertainment programmes by mainstream media organisations. He was of the view that the real problems facing the nation were primarily socio-economic in nature and by extending coverage to films and entertainment instead of focusing on issues like that of malnutrition and poverty, the media was being unmindful of the nation's needs.

It becomes important to analyse how entertainment coverage affect news value. The programmes being aired on television are not merely a piece of content with information; it has a certain news value which affects opinion, views, mindset and understanding of the audiences. It is certain that entertainment broadcast affects several aspect of human life. Its implications are indeed manifold. It is not about titillating senses of the viewer, rather shaping their attitude and thinking.

Researches proved that in prime time news, the content focus is mainly on politics (17.16%), sports (15.67%), film and entertainment (11.04%), crime (7.14%) and international affairs (8.56%) during 2005 to 2013. It is noteworthy that news channels carry entertainment and crime shows besides giving them prime time coverage. The Indian broadcasting industry is presently a major contributor to the national economy and is currently witnessing rapid technological advancement with the introduction of new applications. Convergence of media technologies is on the rise coupled with a steep growth in the number of news channels. Foreign media outlets have also shown inkling in investing more in the Indian media. The opportunities at hand are encouraging media organisations based in the country to experiment more and more with their business formula, i.e., content for audiences, *viz.*, content for business.

Apart from prime time coverage, different programmes are produced, keeping in mind the slots for audiences. Almost everywhere there is a programme based on TV serials and their happenings. These programmes air small snippets from the previous day's episode of some of the famous shows on television. Sometimes they also conduct special interviews with the leading faces of the small screen. Such programmes serve a dual purpose. They build the existing popularity of certain soaps, while simultaneously diverging some audience traffic from different channels to their own.

For the specific purpose, news channels have come up with another form of entertainment news presentation where comedy is the prime source of the programme. Raju Srivastava's Comedy Express and Gajodhar Bhaiya on Aaj Tak were broadcasted on prime time, in which Raju used to make fun of the daily news in the former. Politics, crime, sports and entertainment news are the main targets of such programmes. Similarly, 2G on IBN7 and Haste Raho on News 24 are of the similar kind. Such presentation deteriorates the news value and degrades the actual news.

Although entertainment news does not carry the traditional news values which hard news stories command, they fulfill the initial two parameters of serving the interests of the reporter and the producer as well as of the company. Through coverage of promotional exercises, channels seek to establish their own value and brand in the market. If a particular celebrity appears more often than not on a particular channel, then it is the reputation of the channel that is bound to gain from the same.

As far as news value is concerned, celeb value is another thing which clicks mind in entertainment news. News creators have not been able to classify the type of news intermixed. For instance, Monica Bedi, the alleged girlfriend of the underworld don Abu Salem, was more in news when Salem was arrested. The seriousness of the news was somewhere lost with Monica Bedi being eye candy for the media. Monica Bedi received higher coverage in entertainment news than Abu Salem in crime news. Recently, another Bollywood actress Mamta Kulkarni was arrested in Kenya for drug trafficking and media repeated the history. The intensity of celebrity is always placed above that of news. Somewhere down the line, the societal values are ignored and voyeurism among the people is served.

An entertainment editor of a famous news channel stated that in the realm of entertainment news, "News is what benefits you or your boss. If it doesn't benefit your boss then how will it benefit the company? If it is not up to the mark on these two parameters then think about news value." Obviously, the content that is broadcasted in the name of entertainment news is far away from the values of the news.

According to Althaus *et al.* (2011), what journalists call "news value" is an important factor in the media selection process. They go on to note that the standard elements of news value include timeliness, novelty, geographic proximity, familiarity, audience impact and drama. These factors are important elements of the triage process that news organisations use to determine the stories to include in scarce news space; the greater the news value of a story, greater is the likelihood that it will survive the triage. While all components of news value are important, they note that drama and novelty are especially important. Sometimes the novelty and drama of developments are so striking that their news value trumps other influences on the media selection process, thus offsetting the distortions that may result from institutional or contextual factors.

Despite all the jargon, the audiences continue to like softer stories pertaining to cinema and entertainment, which allow them to get a sense of happiness and leisure. The consumption of such news becomes a societal must as it often shapes conversations among peer groups who are awed by the lifestyle of their much cherished artists. Reportage on such events influences audiences and arrests their attention at once. The scene of a mob awaiting the sight of Amitabh Bachchan on his birthday is appealing to the television audience as it provides them the opportunity to be in close proximity to their stars, although such proximity is fuelled by technology.

Entertainment reporting affects on voyeurism of the viewers in the terms of revealing facts about a hidden star. They feel proud whenever they find them close to their own behavioural patterns. In entertainment reporting for the same, they try to present scripted lifestyle of stars.

Another major cause of entertainment coverage is its production nature. Producers require less effort to produce it in very minimal budget. Media organisations are profit-driven organisations with a huge investment in infrastructure, machines and human resources. That's why they feel the need to cut down their production cost at each and every step wherever possible. Obviously the production of television programmes needs greater involvement of human resources. Hundreds of reporters, journalists, technicians and other crew members are required to carry out the task with utmost proficiency. Production of entertainment news is a very easy task for producers. They need not go around collecting footage as it is required in any other formate. For the production of news content, feed is the most important material, which is edited, packaged and broadcasted over different platforms. An entertainment news producer need not send his crew on the field every time to gather information. A lot of soft material, promos and other stocks is available with appropriate edit and background store. For content like Comedy Express, they need only an anchor link to present the programme as it is. Even programmes like debates, with a very low budget production for the organisation, requires more human hours than an entertainment production. This could be one of the reasons because of which entertainment shows are able to trump over serious discussions on politics and current affairs.

Normally the PR team of any film produces promos and teasers to provide them to media. It is a readymade material for the news broadcasters to incorporate in the news content. Without any hustle, they have material in hand so as to design a programme. This enables news organisations to manage their 24x7 news cycle efficiently. Although the footage available for every competitor is same, the producer evolves innovation to attract audiences. Repeat coverage done in accordance to PR team is beneficial for the reporter or his boss or to the organisation at some other levels; for instance, celebrities give promos and, statements in the favour of the organisation, which provide an edge over audiences. The core mantra of the entertainment beat is premised around the saying, "You scratch my back, and I'll scratch yours." The active collusion of celebrities, journalists and PR provide the recipe for mutual publicity and gain.

Bollywood, as the Hindi film industry is popularly known, is the largest contributor to the industry's revenue, followed by the South Indian film industry and other language cinema industries such as Bengali, Bhojpuri, Marathi and Gujarati. Although the country's film entertainment industry is the largest in the world in terms of the number of films produced (around 900) and its theatrical admissions (around 3 billion), it continues to be small in size in terms of revenue, mainly due to low ticket realisation and occupancy levels. Film producers adapt several PR strategies to publicise their work. They plan campaigns for pre-release knock to the audiences and increasing their curiosity. These initiatives are aimed at maximising audience turnout at film theatres. *RA.One* perhaps had the first organised 360-degree campaign for an Indian film and had more than 25 brands associated with it in various capacities. The film's leading attraction was Bollywood superstar Shah Rukh Khan, whose popularity arguably helped in amassing the large number of brands.

"The All Is Well-Reliance Life Insurance" campaign launched as part of the promotional campaign of the film, *3 Idiots* broke across television channels, radio stations and hoardings featuring the lead actors of the film. The advertisement used the proposition, 'Jab Hai Saath Reliance Life Insurance, All Is Well', to convey its messages to the masses through 50 television channels and 19,000 spots in a matter of five weeks. On the radio, it took up 11,000 spots over 50 channels covering 35 cities, 50 television channels and 19,000 spots. Mostly entertainment coverage comes from Bollywood and Tollywood—both requires audience recognition after release. Broadcast media stands as the appropriate media vehicle for this purpose.

Bollywood has adopted many strange methods of promoting films. Prominent personalities like Mahesh Bhatt have used propagandas to bring the films into limelight. For the second installment of the popular horror series *Raaz,* popularly known as *Raaz, The Mystery Continues* staring Kangana Ranaut, Emraan Hashmi and Adhyayan Suman, the producer of the film Mr Bhatt claimed in an interview that owing to the horror content of the film, the system crashed thrice during editing. He even claimed of doing puja at the places where the film was shot. Such statements are only promotion strategies of the production house. It serves in the interest of the production house that provides elements to sensitise the news media. During the filming of the same film, the chemistry between the male and female protagonists, that is, Adhyayan Suman and Kangana Ranaut were highlighted by the PR team as a promotion strategy.

The media went gaga over behind the news and broadcasted it in every possible way. Both broke up after release of the film. We have many such instances to quote: Salman Khan is linked to every actress he works with, Ajay Devgan was linked with Kangana Ranaut during the shoot of *Rascals* and *Once Upon A Time in Mumbai*, Katrina Kaif and Ranbir Kapoor were often linked by media and the actress had to break up with her then boyfriend, Salman Khan. This obviously questions media credibility. The broadcaster should not only give information based on legal aspects, but should also take in to accord the ethical parameters of the society. The value of any story is determined by its significance, along with proximity, prominence, timeliness, and human interest. Stories propagated by PR agencies are neither trustworthy, nor they carry any news value in itself though they are broadcasted with complete blow-up.

The promotion of films is also done by studio visits. The star cast visits the studio and special programmes are arranged by the media team. These are generally interview-based programmes where questions related to the film are asked. Although cinema has little to do with news media, it still manage to acquire good media attention. Abhishek Bachchan and Rani Mukerji were given role of news presenter on NDTV during release of their film *Bunty aur Bubli*, senior Bachchan were also on screen to present news at the time of *Rann*. Celebrities come on screen with an intention to promote their film and news organisations are putting forth presenting that information as news content; the organisation needs to identify the difference between film promotion and entertainment news. No doubt such information is acceptable to the masses, but its value remains negligible.

Tie-ups with popular brands is also done as a part of co-branding and increasing the films credibility. Screens flood with such advertisements where the film star cast promote their film *vis-à-vis* products. Jhandu Balm (Salman Khan's *Dabangg*), Astral Pipes (Salman Khan's *Dabangg*-2), Royal Challenge (Ajay Devagan's *Action Jackson*) and Dollar (Akshay Kumar's *Boss*) are a few examples where commercials have been used to create a credible environment for the film. The actual list is too lengthy to reproduce in full. Speaking of the phenomena of tie-ups with popular brands, one of the biggest examples is that of FMCG-ointment Jhandu Balm, which featured very prominently in a popular film *Dabangg*, which starred Salman Khan. Jhandu Balm, which once had a firm command, had lost its presence in the FMCG market. But when it was featured as part of the super hit song, 'Munni Badnaam', its sales soared by 30 per cent within a matter of weeks. This tie-up came like a blessing for the ointment company.

Many brands and companies sponsor certain scenes in films, where their brand ambassador-actors promote the product. Thus, innovation and creativity work wonders as compared to conventional methods of advertising and marketing, as it has a more powerful appeal to the masses. Co-branding, as a result of film promotion, is the key factor of slot regulation over 24x7 news channels. The budget set to spend on publicity of the film and that particular brand both gives an edge over the number of slots that can be purchased for the promotion. Thus they increase the degree of exposures.

Not only the number of slots, with larger amount for advertisement, they are capable to negotiate with the service, provider i.e., news broadcaster to give appropriate mileage to the brand and product.

Innovative marketing strategies adopted by film producers attract media houses to make news on the same due to its 'wow' coefficient. It is capable of pulling audiences into the content and holding them for a while. It serves the purpose of both broadcasters and film producers. Innovative marketing can be discussed through some marketing strategies adopted by the Indian film producers in 2008. Shahrukh Khan's *Rab Ne Bana Di Jodi* and Aamir Khan's *Ghajini* were being released within a span of two weeks, but an innovative move by Aamir Khan completely overshadowed the other film.

This strategy was reportedly borne out of the "perfectionist's" mind himself. At every ticket window in every theatre, when audiences went to buy tickets for any film, they saw people sitting with 'Ghajini hairstyles' selling tickets. This really influenced the visiting audiences, and led to a spontaneous buying of *Ghajini's* tickets, thereby helping its business to score way over other films.

Obviously, this innovation got *Ghajini* a huge media coverage as well as the story about ticket selling to theater attendant got media coverage. Reporters were enthusiastically interrogating hall attendants to know the reasons and in all this *Ghajini* was being promoted. A similar innovation was used during the release of the film *3 Idiots*, as films props like benches were put across theatres. Not only the producer of the films comes with innovations but programme producers of different news broadcasters are also following the same pattern due to common feed by the PR team of the production. Before the release of the Bollywood film, *Oye Lucky! Lucky Oye*!, Zee News came out with a promo that Bunty Chor (the character on whom the film was largely centred upon) was caught on camera and that the viewers could watch that full episode on their entertainment show. They propagated the episode as a real one, but it appeared on screen in the form of a common, show like a Conversation with the Cast and Crew of *Oye Lucky! Lucky Oye*! The programme was dramatised in the form of a road chase by the police to catch Bunty.

All these innovative marketing moves yielded special results for the film business and proved to be successful PR campaigns helping the businesses of different films. Broadcasters and producers both were in a win-win situation due to the double whammy. Television industry has a history of endorsement of content, which has nothing to do with news media content. The news industry has always promoted entertainment news with Bollywood masala. In earlier instances, we have seen Bollywood stars promoting their films on shows like *Sansani* which telecasts on ABP news (earlier Star News). Same is the case with the longest running television show *Aap Ki Adalat*, where Aamir Khan promoted *3 idiots* and Salman Khan promoted *Dabangg* and *Jai Ho*. *Tarak Mehta Ka Oolta Chasma* and Kapil Sharma's *Comedy Nights* are similar shows that have given rise to the intermixing of different kinds of media content which needs a new classification. The idea of such intermixing is not the need of the hour, rather it is the need of the producers and advertisers for garnering TRPs (television rating points). This intermixing makes huge negative impact on news value and the quality deteriorates.

Controversies are another hot stuff for media industry, where they can produce programmes with the help of promos, can call affected/involved parties for live debates; the sensational pinch of the programme can be an attention-grabbing button for the audiences. Controversy over *PK* is the best example of the attention-grabbing coefficient; debate over maligning *versus* freedom of expression is on air along with a huge crowd is on booking window.

Box 10.1

Indian Cinema: Progression and Parlance

1896	• 7 July 1896, Cinema debuted in India with the brothers Auguste and Louis Lumière unveiling six short, silent films at Watson's Hotel in Bombay.
1913	• May 1913; India's first full length feature film, a mythological epic —*Raja Harishchandra* — produced by Dadasaheb Phalke, was commercially released in Bombay.
1931	• 14 March 1931; Ardeshir Irani directed and released the first 'talking' movie — *Alam Ara*. It was a commercial success and 'talkies' were born.
1937	• Ardeshir Irani produced the country's first colour feature film, *Kisan Kanya*, but the black and white era continued till the 1950s, when Eastman Color became dominant.
1950-60	• This emerged as the golden age of Indian cinema with hits such as Raj Kapoor's *Awaara* (1951), Guru Dutt's trilogy that included *Pyaasa* (1957) and K. Asif's *Mughal-e-Azam* (1960).
1970s	• The 1970s signalled the rise of modern Bollywood featuring Rajesh Khanna, Dharmendra and Shashi Kapoor. Romantic, song-and-dance films like *Aradhana* , *Jewel Thief* and *Anand* were released.
	• Modern parallel cinema or 'art cinema' was also born, with directors like Shyam Benegal, Govind Nihalani and Vijaya Mehta, and films like *Ankur* and *Nishant*. Film Finance Corp. gave financial support.
1975	• The release of Sholay brought Amitabh Bachchan, and star power, to the pinnacle. The film ran for a record 286 weeks in a theatre in Bombay. Made on a budget of ₹ 2 crore, the film grossed ₹ 15 crore. This film was loaded with promotional song 'item number' Mehbooba - Mehbooba.
1990s	• Indian cinema embraced technology like Dolby digital sound, special effects and choreography to enhance production quality and consumer experience. Overseas distribution of Indian movies became an organised business.
1993	• The launch of private television networks created a huge demand for film content. Films and Bollywood now account for more than 30 per cent of entertainment television programming, while TV networks are a major source of film revenue.
1997	• Rise of multiplex culture gave a new dimension to the business.

contd...

.contd...

2000	• The government granted 'industry' status to the film business and the IDBI Act was amended to cover the entertainment industry for institutional funding
2000-03	• International media groups, like Time Warner and Sony Pictures, entered Indian film-making. Indian producers like Mukta Arts raised fund through Initial Public Offerings (IPOs).
2008	• *Ghajini*, remake of a Tamil film, became the first to cross the ₹ 100-crore mark in gross box-office revenues. (Total collection of ₹ 190 crore) thus a corelation is seen between promotional activities and box office revenue.

Source: Businessworld Magazine

The Indian television industry dominated the media and entertainment landscape in India. As per a FICCI-KPMG Indian Media and Entertainment Industry Report 2014, the television industry in India, which was estimated at ₹41,720 crore (US$ 6.94 billion) in 2013, is projected to increase at a compound annual growth rate (CAGR) of 16.2 per cent over 2013-2018, to reach ₹88,500 crore (US$ 14.72 billion) by 2018. The growth of TV industry was 12.7 per cent over 2012. Television penetration is only around 60 per cent in India and hence there a is great scope for the industry to grow exponentially. The cost of skilled professional, technicians and production is high enough. To meet these challenges, innovative strategies are of utmost need.

Broadcasters derive revenues primarily from two sources *viz*., advertisement and subscription, in addition to content monetisation through arrangements with other broadcasting platforms. Advertisements are the lifeline of media organisations and the chief source of their revenue. The advertisement revenues contribute to around 70-80 per cent of the total revenues for majority of the broadcasters in India (exception ZEEL), and the share of subscription revenues remains low. The leakages in subscription revenue currently deprive the channels of a significant and relatively more stable source of revenue, with only 20 per cent of the same currently accruing to the broadcasters. In contrast, the broadcasters in developed markets of western countries enjoy a much larger share of the subscription revenues (35-40%). However, the overdependence on advertisement revenue has many a times been criticised by scholars as having directly influenced the editorial policy of the concerned media organisation.

Now it is important to understand how entertainment coverage affects news value. The programme aired on TV screen is not merely a piece of information; it affects opinion, views, mindset and understanding of the audiences. Obviously an entertainment broadcast affects all aspect of human life. Its implications are indeed manifold. It is not simply about titillating the senses of the viewers, rather shaping their attitude and thinking.

Role of that broadcaster is not to give information based on legal aspects, but also to consider the ethical parameters of the society. The value of a story is judged by the associated significance, timeliness, prominence, proximity, bizarreness, conflict and human interest. Although the entertainment news can be proved to a valuable content, the value of the same is definitely not trustworthy.

In his paper "Designing Credibility: An Analysis of the Visual Aesthetics of Television News", Zane Van Dusen wrote that reporters have always been placed in front of very realistic backdrops. Whenever reporting from the field, reporters are posed in front of major icons, which already have some significance to the viewer (White House, Capitol Hill, overlooking a Middle Eastern city). Even if the story is actually taking place inside the halls of Capitol Hill, "the reporter must leave 'the scene' in order to locate himself 'symbolically'." These carefully planned backdrops are used to give the report "visual authenticity." They convince us as viewers that the reporter is truly at a location, which seems familiar to us, and he or she has the latest information on the situation. This is nothing except increase in news value of the content. In the case of entertainment news, we don't normally care about such specific coverage.

Since time immemorial, journalism has been viewed as a form of public service. The many giants of journalism whom we remember with much pride today were vocal proponents of missionary journalism. Their lives were dedicated to using journalism as an instrument to raise their voices and concerns against the unjust practices prevalent in society. Indian journalism went through the same ideological phase. The press was used as a tool to counter the imperial rule in British India. Leaders like Mahatma Gandhi greatly understood the power of communication and they saw newspapers as an important device using which the freedom movement could be given further impetus. This led to journalism being principally associated with socio-political issues and other subjects of economic concern.

However, it was not that entertainment news was alien to Indian journalism, prior to the rise of 24x7 news channels. The first official newspaper to have been floated in India was *Hicky's Gazette,* which is known to have published news concerning affairs and gossip regarding British officers. The 21st century media has only institutionalised entertainment news in a big way. The reason for the same is simple. Entertainment news has emerged as a sellable commodity, not merely in the realm of prime time coverage but also coverage during other times. The trend cuts across linguistic and cultural barriers as visible from the dominance of entertainment news in both Hindi and English media.

The emergence of entertainment news has certainly raised ethical issues. The criticism is two-fold. While some accuse media organisations of ignoring the real-world problems and dealing in the reel world, others condemn news organisations for parroting the briefs of PR professionals during their coverage of entertainment news. Notwithstanding the criticism, the editors of mainstream media view entertainment news as easy to gather and telecast. What remains to be seen is how long entertainment news will continue to deliver favourable profits to news media owners.

References

Althaus, Scott L., Nathaniel Swigger, Svitlana Chernykh, David J. Henry, Sergio C. Wals, and Christopher Tiwald (2011). "Assumed Transmission in Political Science: A Call for Bringing Description Back", in *Journal of Politics* 73(4): 1065-80.

Anon (2014). "The Economist is Wrong, Print Media is Declining in India too by Anant Rangaswami", *http://firstbiz.firstpost.com/corporate/the-economist-is-wrong-print-media-is-declining-in-india-too-20791.html*). Retrieved 26 December 2014.

Businessworld (2013). *Business World* 40-41.

Dusen, Zane Van. (2014). "Designing Credibility An Analysis of the Visual Aesthetics of Television News". terribleinformation.org. Retrieved 26 December 2014 (*http://www.terribleinformation.org/zane/files/DesigningCredibility.pdf*).

http://www.clinecenter.illinois.edu/ (2014). "Media Data And Social Science Research: Problems and Approaches". Retrieved December 26, 2014 (*http://www.clinecenter.illinois.edu/publication/white/speed/documents/MediaDataandSocialScienceResearch.pdf*).

Indianmirror.com (2014). 'Indian Television Industry at a Glance in 2012-2013, Television Industry in India, Television Industry, Television Industries, TV Industry'. Retrieved December 26, 2014 (*http://www.indianmirror.com/indian-industries/2013/television-2013.html*).

Mbaskool.com (2014). "Innovative Marketing: Movies, Magic and Marvel | Business Article | MBA Skool-Study.Learn.Share." Retrieved December 26, 2014 (*http://www.mbaskool.com/business-articles/marketing/150-innovative-marketing-movies-magic-marvel.html*).

Rangaswami, Anant (2014). "The Story Behind the Amazing Marketing of 3 Idiots". Rediff. Retrieved December 26, 2014 (*http://business.rediff.com/slide-show/2010/aug/06/slide-show-1-the-story-behind-the-amazing-marketing-of-3-idiots.htm#5*).

www.icra.in (2011). "Indian Television Broadcasting Industry: Recent Developments". Retrieved December 26, 2014 (*http://www.icra.in/Files/ticker/Media, Quarterly%20Note,%20July%202011.pdf*).

11

ALOK SRIVASTAVA

Corruption Reporting in TV News Channels in India

Corruption is not an alien word. At every level, from policy makers to common citizens, from institution to individuals, from rich to poor, from law enforcement agency to community, from developed countries to developing countries, no one is untouched from the affects of corruption. Yet, defining corruption is difficult. People from time to time have defined corruption in various ways. Broadly, corruption stands for those illegal practices, in which citizens or organisations bribe officials in return for awarding permissions, contracts, or to escape punishment or fines for offenses they committed. In short, corruption is to obtain privileges against law of the land or the rules.

India is the world's largest democracy. A vibrant and diverse mass media is an important pillar of democracy in the country. The independence of the media facilitates adherence to democratic norms. Article 19 of the Constitution of India confers the right to freedom of speech and expression to all citizens of the country and to the media as well.

The present chapter however aims to focus only on reporting of corruption in media. But before we go into the history of reporting on corruption and do a trend analysis of the extent and type of reporting on corruption practiced in India, it is important to understand the length and breadth of the prevalence of corruption here. This will help to understand the sectors, components, modus operandi and key players involved in corrupt practices and their influence, if any on the reporting on corruption.

Key players or stakeholders play an important and critical role in deciding the content and frequency of reporting of corruption by media.

With penetration of mass media up to the village level as well as presence of corruption right from national administrative set up to the village service delivery system and across almost all spheres of life, it is important to first understand the magnitude of corruption. This is because magnitude of corruption along with the key players decide the extent of reporting on corruption-based news in mass media.

Before we analyse television news channels' reporting on corruption, let us understand what all comes under corrupt practices and how deep it is rooted in our society. At national or province or even societal level, to measure the extent of corruption prevalant is easier said than done. Based on the experience of undertaking several studies to measure corruption,[1] a lot of complexities are involved in measuring corruption.

In fact, many scholars argue that corruption is a broader phenomenon, or rather, a hardly definable set of phenomena, including achieving several advances through personal networking; paying gratitude money or giving gifts for usual services that are already reimbursed from customers or state resources (The Hungarian Gallup Institute, 1999).

In fact, the search for effective methods of combating corruption has led to an increasingly wide recognition that corruption is fundamentally a problem of governance. Corruption thrives where states are too weak to control their own bureaucrats, to protect property and contract rights, and to provide the institutions that underpin an effective rule of law (The World Bank, 2000). According to Pavarala (1996) and Shleifer and Vishny (1993), corruption is a major hindrance to governance, development and a threat to democratisation.

---

1. Author is associated with CMS, a social research organisation in New Delhi, India and is a senior member of the team which has undertaken India Corruption Study annually for last one decade across different states (provinces) of India.

On the other hand, many believe that corruption has become a 'fact of life' and beyond redemption not only in developing or emerging, economies but in developed nations as well. As argued by Girling (1997) corruption does not disappear as countries develop and modernise instead it takes on new forms. In fact corruption slows down development. As Planning Commission of India had in its 10th Plan report noted: "Corruption is most endemic and entrenched manifestation of poor governance in Indian society, so much so it has almost become an accepted reality and a way of life". In the 11th Five Year Plan too, it somewhat reiterated that 'good governance' is not possible without addressing corruption in the various manifestations, especially in the context of basic services.[2]

For making it easier to understand, corruption could broadly be categorised as one, which directly involves the common citizen and second, which could be identified as institutional corruption. However, in both the cases, the ultimate sufferer is the common citizen. While, in the first type of corruption, citizens are compelled to use illegal/unofficial means. For instance, in order to get a contract from the government for supply of food items or drugs to government supply centre or health centres, if illegal means are adopted by 'greasing the palms' of bureaucrats or/and politicians, the contractors/suppliers make all efforts to 'recover' the spent amount on bribe by either overcharging the customer or diverting the stocks to open market, thus gaining much more than what was paid as bribe. The 'transaction' between contractor (supplier) and service providers is an institutional or systemic corruption. While creation of false scarcity of essential items by diverting them to open market is another form of corruption wherein the common citizens suffer as they have to buy at higher price, which otherwise would have been available at subsidised rate or free of cost in public service delivery centres. In India, many instances were reported where foodgrains were diverted from warehouses to open market instead to avail the services, while in the second scenario, the institutions, through their representatives, pay bribe or use influence to make the rules and law

2. TII-CMS India Corruption Study 2007.

'favourable', which ultimately is passed on to users of the services provided by these institutions.

In the first type of corruption, identified as petty corruption, citizens have to either bribe, or take help of some influential person or middlemen to avail the services from a government department. This could be the scenario even for getting the prescribed application/ registration forms, or even for medicines otherwise available free of cost or to get admission in government-run schools. For media therefore to report on such incidents have to rely on self-reporting by citizens, or of late as it has become popular, opt for 'sting operation' to trap corrupt officials and practices through audio or video recordings.

Identifying types of corruption as well as purposes or reasons for paying bribe or using contacts is important to improve the efficiency of service delivery in government services. Mass media has a very important role to play in this. For media, it is equally important to assess the quantum of corruption as it helps to analyse and identify the extent to which corrupt practices are deep-rooted in government service delivery system, which in turn is plaguing the growth and development process of the individuals, community and country.

Contributing Factors

One of the prerequisite, in fact, is to identify the factors contributing to the cause. In case of public services, service delivery and corruption are interlinked. These factors could be broadly categorised as one, transaction related, where the kind of prevailing service delivery system and nature of the service as well as availability of alternative, are some key factors facilitating corruption. The second factor, which contributes to corrupt practices, is related to process or the system of a particular public service. More often it has been noticed that unclear job responsibilities, lack of accountability and non-existence of monitoring system in a particular department, assist in 'grooming' of corrupt practices. The third is due to non-clarity or indecisiveness on policy related issues for improving service delivery. In short, these factors could be categorised as: a) at policy level; b) at process level; and c) at implementation or execution level.

Corruption Reporting in TV News

Without any doubt, one can say that corruption, particularly in public services, has been brought to limelight by media from time to time since India got independence. Media during neo-independence era was primarily press or print media. The jeep scandal in 1948 was the first major corruption case in independent India that became public. Since then almost every year, corruption-based stories have been reported by print media. During that time, as we all know newspaper was the main source of media along with radio. All India Radio (AIR), the government owned only broadcaster in India, was the only source of news-based information, not only in Independent India, but till date. Even presently, private radio channels are not allowed to broadcast news bulletins. Post 1997, under Prasar Bharti, AIR and Doordarshan may have attained some autonomy and independence to decide the contents of the programmes including news. This was missing earlier as both were working as media units under the Ministry of Information & Broadcasting (MoI&B), Government of India.[3] Presence of television and news channels in particular was nowhere in India until early 1980s.

Initiation of the television era in India could be identified and associated with Asian Games held in 1982 in New Delhi. Gradually, television as a medium started penetrating in to smaller towns and then to villages of India. Until the beginning of last decade of 20th century (1990s), Doordarshan (DD), the public broadcasting agency had monopoly as far as television channel and programmes are concerned. Being under control of the government, the programme content including the news content was to a large extent closely monitored by the government of the day, and so the reporting of corruption-based news items. Early 1990s saw the entry of private television channels, also known as Cable and Satellite (C&S) channels. C&S channels started with entertainment programme channels, but

3. Accessed from *http://prasarbharati.gov.in*

soon Indian viewers had the privilege of watching news on television telecast by a private television channel. The content was also more 'independent'. The launch of Star TV and Zee TV further enhanced the spread of cable TV and so does the reporting pattern in news bulletin. With channels becoming 24x7 and exclusive news channels being launched by all major media houses, the news reporting too saw a drastic change...for good or bad is for the viewers to decide, but it did influence the demand for content. News channels had two options—one, to bring more and more 'new' news or two, to keep on repeating the same news again and again until the news item has become stale. The first option definitely needed more resources both in terms of human and financial, as well as making efforts to search for the relevant and worth reporting news items. Unlike local stingers in case of print media, television news reporters were and in most cases even now continue to be stationed in major cities and towns. As a consequence, despite news channels, claiming to be 'national', restricted their news reporting to national capital region and metros as well as neo-metro cities. The focus of reporting too, due to the reasons like 'saleability' or 'sensational', focused more on scams and scandals and less on corruption faced by common citizens. Thanks to politicians and to an extent the bureaucracy, activities related to monetary corruption or unfair practices or nepotism have surfaced at regular intervals. Events like Bofors gun deal, St. Kitts forgery, Harshad Mehtra Securities scam, Telecom, Telgi stamp paper scam, Fodder scam, Uttar Pradesh Ayurveda Scam, Mining, Commonwealth Games, Coal scam, and 3G telecom scam, among many others, have been reported in the news. Over and above this, disproportionate assets acquired by politicians and bureaucrats had also come and keep on coming in the limelight. As a result, the priority for reporters is scams and scandals, rather than for systematic issues and correctives, that need to be pursued. The far-off and grass-roots level corruption has hardly figured in the news.

Table 11.1

Top Scams

Year	*Scams in News*
2008	2G Spectrum
2009	Satyam Corporate
2010	Commonwealth Games
2011	Cash-for-vote
2011	Lavasa Township
2012	Coal Mine Allocation
2012	Chopper Purchase
2012	Tatra Truck Purchase
2012	Adarsh Housing
2012	Black Money
2013	Cricket's Indian Premier League
2013	Saradha Group Financial Irregularity
2014	Vyapam-Medical Education

Source: *India Today* (accessed from http://indiatoday.intoday.in/gallery/scandals-during-uparule/1/4240.html; *http://indiatoday.intoday.in/gallery/upa-govt-9-years-9-scams-sonia-manmohan/1/9401.html*)

The key corruption-related events during last seven years, which were widely covered by television news channels (Table 11.1) reflect the similar practice. At the same time, it would not be wrong to say that these stories form just the tip of an iceberg. If we start listing the entire corruption-based stories at national as well as states, then it could run into pages, and the total money involved would be huge and almost unimaginable.

Most of the corruption stories covered in television news channels involved individuals, but with high profiles and of high magnitude. English channels focused relatively more—both on institutions and individuals; while Hindi news channels focused more on individuals in their coverage of corruption.

In covering corruption, the focus of news media hitherto has been primarily the government, bureaucrats and politicians. But the year 2011 signalled that corporate/private sector too matters for news media, and they were no longer out of bounds from their coverage. This could be one of the reasons for higher percentage share in time devoted for news related to corruption.

The last seven years of television news based on five television news channels' prime time news coverage (7-11 pm) has shown some interesting trends. As far as reporting is concerned, compared to 2010, more self-initiated reporting happened in 2014.[4] Unlike 5-7 years back when it was more of a 'routine reporting' on corruption stories, the television news channels in 2014 had a larger proportion of initiative-based reporting (Table 11.2). It shows positive changes as news channels do their 'homework' and investigate to provide insights to the ongoing stories as well as unearth new ones. Social media too has been handy in providing substantial evidence on the news stories. Undoubtedly, this is a welcome trend and reflects that the TV news channels in India are coming of age; however to an extent only, as two-third of the reporting still follows the routine approach.

The analysis also brings out that corruption involving individuals has got more coverage compared to institutions. This if we compare with the list of scandals (Table 11.1) since 2008, a similar trend emerges which highlights more and more involvement of individuals than institutions in corrupt practices. More individuals getting covered in the news could be due to the fact that initiative-based reporting has zeroed in on the persons responsible for corrupt practices or played key roles within the institution, which engaged in corrupt practices for business gains. News related to prominent politicians, bureaucrats and public figures mainly get covered in individual based stories on corruption. Moreover, 2014 being Parliamentary election year in India, could be the reason for more individual based stories last year, as the potential candidates and their wrong-doings were brought to the public by their opponents. Looking at the last seven years' trend (2008 onwards), one could see that in 2011, following the Anna Hazare movement on Lokpal Bill and corruption, more individual-centric corruption stories, particularly involving politicians and bureaucrats, got highlighted.

4. CMS Media Lab Reports 2010-2014.

This could be the right reason to bring home the point that politicians and bureaucracy need to be covered under Lokpal. Other enabling environment for better and more reporting on corruption at times could be attributed to the Right to Information Act 2005, which although to a little extent only, helped media reporters/journalists to bring in public stories on unfair and corrupt means and illegal practices involving government officials, private players and politicians. However, the use of RTI Act for seeking and getting information was observed to be minuscule.

Table 11.2

TV News Coverage of Corruption Trends for 2010, 2011 and 2014

Corruption Issues	*2010 (January to June) Total Time (in %)*	*2011 (January to June) Total Time (in %)*	*2014 (January to June) Total Time (in %)*
Initiative Based Reporting	15.80	16.65	35.81
Routine Reporting	84.15	83.35	64.19
	100.00	100.00	100.00
Corruption involving Individual	37.01	82.60	68.71
Corruption involving Institutions	62.94	17.40	31.29
	100.00	100.00	100.00
Routine Coverage	69.81	88.58	53.14
Special Coverage	30.16	11.42	46.86
	100.00	100.00	100.00
Public Utilities	33.14	29.74	27.10
Big Bodies	41.97	24.05	38.91
Bureaucracy	24.92	46.21	33.99
	100.00	100.00	100.00
Corruption involving Private Sector	4.61	15.25	44.42
Corruption in Government Bodies/Services	95.35	84.75	55.58
	100.00	100.00	100.00

Source: CMS Media Lab.

A noticeable feature of television news coverage on corruption based stories in 2014 has been a significant increase, almost 10 times than 2010, in stories on private sectors. While such stories reflect upon a clear PPP (public-private-partnership) in corrupt practices as well in India. This however, does not mean that corruption in private sector was less in 2010. Rather reporting or focus on private sector based corruption was comparatively lesser or the presentation of such stories was more tilted towards governments' misdeed and less on role of private players/business houses. With opening of more business opportunities for private players in different sectors, earlier having government monopoly, the corruption involving business houses also came more into limelight. The credit should go to the media investigative reporting along with civil society groups and social activists, both supplementing and complementing each other. But these reporting have not been always impartial or neutral. Media houses are accused of being biased, towards or against, few business houses. Ownership of television channels by different business houses was considered as one of the reasons for giving more time slots to corruption issues involving certain business houses, which are rivals. In short, the proportion of time slots in such cases was directly proportional to the extent of business rivalry, and less on nature and magnitude of corruption involved.

Figure 11.1

Prime Time (7-11 pm) Coverage of Corruption in TV News (2008-2014)

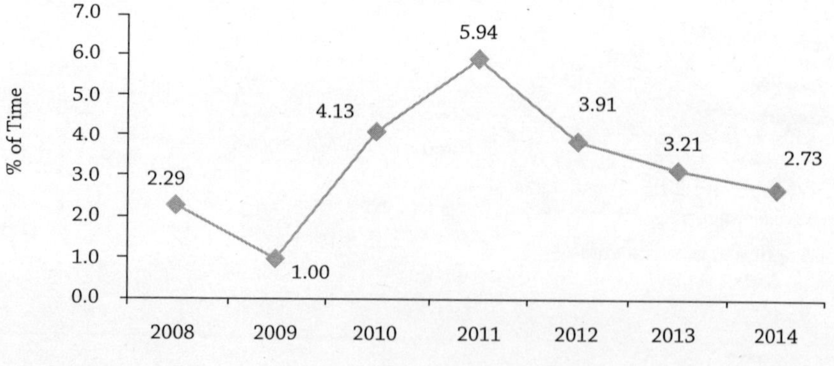

Source: CMS Media Lab.

The peak of corruption related reporting in television was in 2011, the year associated with Anna Hazare movement for Lokpal Bill (Figure 11.1).[5] However, this 'movement' got momentum from the corruption related big stories such as Commonwealth Games (CWG) and 2G Spectrum, which came into limelight in the previous year i.e., 2010. However, by the beginning of the year 2012, this seemed to fizzle out from the priority list of television and the corruption stories revolved against allegations and counter-allegations on these cases. Here and there, however, the 'new' feed for television came through Adarsh Housing society or Haryana land scam involving real estate business house and close relatives of prominent public figures. Thus, in 2012, the average figure of news time again dropped to the similar range of that in 2010, and remained more or less around the percentage range. The year 2013 was also the preparatory year of general elections and a major contributor to stories relating to corruption involving different political parties' government at centre or state levels. Television stories on match-fixing in cricket's Indian Premier League (IPL) too contributed to the corruption coverage in television. What is interesting, as well as disturbing, to notice is that television stories focused more on corruption stories involving any big fish and almost negligible on those affecting the common citizens directly. The television channels may suggest that their coverage was very much relevant (no one is denying in fact) as it has tickle-down affect on facilities and amenities available for common citizens. However, perception of the common citizens about the corruption stories is that all (including media) on the top are involved in corrupt practices and least concerned about the bottom of society's pyramid.

5. CMS Media Lab Analysis: *Face of Corruption in News Media* (different rounds).

Table 11.3

Time Devoted by News Channels on Corruption Related Stories by Issues/Topics

Issues/Topic	*Number of Stories*	*%age of Total Time Given*
Sports	82	29.38
Natural Resource	108	13.11
Black Money	70	10.46
Sting	17	9.29
Education	66	8.39
Health	14	5.10
Real State/Land Allotment	32	4.05
Police	6	4.04
Defence	31	3.47
Financial Firms/Chit Funds	22	3.43
Government Schemes	19	1.77
Elections	7	1.61
Helpline	9	1.39
Judiciary	1	1.29
Electricity	4	0.43
Appointment/Recruitments	7	0.31
Telecom	9	0.47
Others	10	2.03
Total	514	100.00

Source: CMS Media Lab data for January-June 2014 of six TV news channels.

With the practice of putting 'breaking news' every half an hour or so, the amplifying effect of these stories are more on the psyche of citizens. The television news channels have more breaking news now a days than 'non-breaking' news. Now it seems that the practice among television news channels is to tag any news item that is flashed for the first time on their channel as breaking news. So, almost all news seems to be the breaking news at one point or the other. The problem with these stories is that they come like missiles and fizzle out like water bubbles. The retention of serious stories in the mind of viewers has been diluted and minimised. The positive aspect of investigative and initiative-based reporting is that more and more stories are coming to the foreground, but the negative side is that follow-up stories are taking a backseat.

A quick analysis of data available on corruption-based stories in terms of the type of issues/topics given preference between January-June 2014 on six television news channels (Table 11.3), pudicates that the top three issues that dominated were: a) sports which include cricket's IPL related match/spot fixing stories; b) natural resources linked such as mining of coal/sand; and c) black money based corruption stories. On the other citizen-centric issues like education, health, electricity or government schemes, which have more direct implications on the daily lives of common citizens, are not getting adequate coverage as far as corruption-related stories are concerned. May be the stories lack spice or does not involve a public (sic) figure.

The Dilemma and Way Ahead

The irony with more and more reporting of corruption-based stories is that the persons or their supporters involved in corrupt practices also try to dilute the seriousness of such cases by comparing the quantum of the fresh scam and scams that got public. They counter it by claiming that corruption practiced by the opponents is of much higher amount and try to give it either communal colour or cover it by showing a make-believe oppression of leaders who belong to marginalised and vulnerable social groups/caste or religion. For their advantage, they get the space in media, particularly television for putting forward their irrational point of defence. Visuals have better impact and therefore television is a good platform for such practitioners and school of thought.

Television channels, on the other hand, cannot be completely blamed for this as they are supposed to be fair to both the parties. Disadvantage is that officials handling the case cannot and in most of the cases, do not counter the false claims on television due to their holding position of responsibility or the case is in the legal court and hence could go against them as contempt of court. Undoubtedly, the role and responsibility of television therefore increases many folds compared to other mass media such as newspapers and radio on these instances because visuals creates much stronger perception, as well as emotional hype. As has been observed, the culprits or the accused try to create an impression that they are innocent and are suffering due to the media trial conducted by television news channels.

Easy said than practiced, self-regulation seems the only way out. Consensus between different television channels not to go overboard for winning the time-race or viewership-race could be expected. However, as a business entity meant for making profit, they can't completely isolate themselves from this money-gain business, irrespective of the ethical concerns and challenges put before them. Most are aware about these. To their credit, by showing these corruption-based stories on their channels, the television channels have definitely done more good than bad. Need is to make the corruption-based stories more of a serious business and less of as an entertaining one.

References

Girling, J. (1997). *Corruption, Capitalism and Democracy*. London: Routledge.

Pavarala, V. (1996). *Interpreting Corruption: Elite Perspectives in India*. New Delhi: Sage.

Sheifer, A. and R.W. Vishny (1993). "Corruption", *The Quarterly Journal of Economics* 108(3): 599-617.

Thakurta, P.G. and K.S. Reddy (2013). "Paid News: How Corruption in the Indian Media is Undermining Democracy", *Real Politik* 8(10).

The Hungarian Gallup Institute (1999). "Basic Methodological Aspects of Corruption Measurement: Lessons Learned From The Literature and the Pilot Study", (December 1999) in UNODCCP and UNICRI. March.

The World Bank (2000). *Measuring Governance, Corruption, and State Capture*. The World Bank Group.

Annexures

Annexures

TV News Content Trends 2005-2014 At a Glance

Annexure Table A-1.1

TV News Trends 2005-2007

Story Topic	*% of News Time*		
	2005	*2006*	*2007*
Accident and Natural Disaster	4.80	1.30	1.72
Agriculture	0.10	0.50	0.19
Arts, Culture and Heritage	1.10	3.50	0.69
Business and Economy	6.30	6.30	4.75
Civic Issue	4.10	2.20	1.12
Crime	9.40	10.50	11.06
Corruption	0.70	0.30	0.44
Education	1.10	0.90	0.69
Election	4.40	0.60	4.34
Environment and Wildlife	0.40	0.50	0.88
Fashion and Lifestyle	0.70	0.70	0.25
Film and Entertainment	6.10	11.50	15.97
Health and Medicine	1.20	2.20	0.85
Human Interest	1.70	4.40	7.69
International Affairs	8.60	5.10	7.54
Law and Order	1.30	1.10	3.58
Legal	6.90	7.70	5.12
Media	-	0.20	0.33
National Politics	11.60	7.50	4.25
National Security and Defence	3.20	5.50	3.53
Others	3.20	1.30	1.23
Public Policy and Governance	2.60	1.30	1.03
Religion	1.60	1.00	2.11
Science and Technology	0.40	0.40	0.68
Sports	10.70	19.20	16.99
State Politics	7.10	3.70	2.65
Weather	0.70	0.40	0.32
Total	100.00	100.00	100.00

Notes: 1. Figures are based on prime time (7-11 pm) coverage of 6 national news channels.

2. Figures are percentage of total news time of 6 national news channels.

3. News channels–Aaj Tak, DD News, NDTV India, Sahara Samay, Star News and Zee News.

Annexure Table A-2.1

Year Wise TV News Content Trends 2008-2014

Story Topic	*% of News Time*						
	2008	*2009*	*2010*	*2011*	*2012*	*2013*	*2014*
Accident and Natural Disaster	1.77	2.48	3.39	2.27	1.95	3.80	2.76
Agriculture	0.29	0.18	0.19	0.09	0.08	0.05	0.18
Arts, Culture and Heritage	0.62	0.88	0.65	1.03	0.83	0.85	1.13
Business and Economy	7.76	6.59	4.09	4.47	4.22	3.34	2.54
Civic Issue	1.31	1.44	2.24	7.30	5.55	3.30	1.89
Corruption	0.29	1.00	4.13	5.94	3.91	3.21	2.73
Crime	4.61	4.86	5.74	5.16	6.63	8.31	3.92
Education	0.66	0.85	0.51	0.60	0.63	0.69	1.48
Environment and Wildlife	0.77	1.53	1.29	0.84	0.65	0.32	0.75
Fashion and Life Style	0.27	0.13	0.31	0.30	0.20	0.12	0.11
Film and Entertainment	13.44	10.13	12.74	9.72	10.16	9.58	7.08
Health and Medicine	1.01	1.87	1.19	1.00	1.00	1.06	1.20
Human Interest	2.48	2.09	1.97	2.74	2.11	2.15	1.35
International Affairs	9.77	12.38	8.14	9.29	7.37	8.83	11.12
Law and Order	2.98	2.04	2.95	1.07	1.03	1.47	1.15
Legal	3.83	1.91	3.62	2.64	2.08	3.12	1.64
Media	0.44	0.45	0.62	0.67	0.48	0.44	0.53
National Politics	6.42	7.27	8.56	13.15	19.04	20.74	16.58
National Security and Defence	9.35	4.98	4.08	3.72	3.10	3.52	2.12
Others	1.73	2.87	4.73	1.48	1.29	1.80	1.20
Public Policy and Governance	1.55	2.31	4.26	4.33	3.01	3.74	4.52
Religion	1.82	1.09	1.23	0.60	0.32	0.59	0.66
Science and Technology	1.53	0.93	0.69	0.61	0.94	0.55	0.49
Sports	20.97	16.03	17.93	16.09	13.06	10.04	5.96
Election	2.22	10.69	0.87	1.69	7.23	4.25	22.18
State Politics	1.85	2.40	3.04	2.84	2.42	3.64	4.28
Weather	0.26	0.59	0.86	0.34	0.70	0.50	0.45
Total	100.00	100.00	100.00	100.00	100.00	100.00	100.00

Notes: 1. Figures are based on prime time (7-11 pm) coverage of 6 national news channels.

2. Figures are percentage of total news time of 6 national news channels.

3. News channels–Aaj Tak, CNN IBN, DD News, NDTV 24x7, Star News/ABP News and Zee News.

Annexure Table A-3.1

Channel-wise TV News Content Trends 2005-2007

January-December 2005	*% of News Time*						
Story Topic	*Aaj Tak*	*Sahara Samay*	*Star News*	*Zee News*	*NDTV India*	*DD News*	*Total*
Accident and Natural Disaster	4.00	4.30	4.10	4.90	4.80	6.40	4.80
Agriculture	0.00	0.10	0.10	0.00	0.10	0.10	0.10
Arts, Culture and Heritage	0.80	1.60	0.70	1.00	1.40	0.90	1.10
Business and Economy	5.10	3.10	3.20	2.20	3.60	18.70	6.30
Civic Issue	3.50	4.00	6.80	5.20	4.50	2.00	4.10
Crime	10.50	8.70	13.40	11.00	12.20	2.80	9.40
Corruption	1.30	0.40	0.80	0.60	0.90	0.20	0.70
Education	1.00	1.10	1.40	1.30	1.20	0.70	1.10
Election	6.20	3.70	2.40	5.60	3.90	4.70	4.40
Environment and Wildlife	0.20	0.50	0.40	0.30	0.40	0.50	0.40
Fashion and Lifestyle	0.90	1.20	0.50	1.00	0.60	0.20	0.70
Film and Entertainment	7.10	5.50	8.80	4.50	6.70	4.60	6.10
Health and Medicine	1.60	1.00	1.50	1.40	1.00	1.10	1.20
Human Interest	1.50	2.40	2.40	1.70	1.40	0.60	1.70
International Affairs	7.40	8.80	6.00	8.40	5.90	13.40	8.60
Law and Order	1.10	1.60	1.50	1.10	1.80	1.00	1.30
Legal	6.90	8.10	6.10	7.60	9.60	3.80	6.90
National Politics	12.00	12.00	8.80	11.30	11.20	13.20	11.60
National Security and Defence	2.90	4.10	2.60	4.20	2.80	2.50	3.20
Others	2.80	2.80	3.30	3.60	2.30	4.30	3.20
Public Policy and Governance	2.00	1.80	2.00	2.90	3.00	4.00	2.60
Religion	1.20	2.00	1.20	2.70	1.40	0.90	1.60
Science and Technology	0.30	0.40	0.40	0.30	0.30	0.60	0.40
Sports	10.00	12.90	14.90	8.60	9.30	8.00	10.70
State Politics	8.80	7.20	5.80	8.20	8.80	4.50	7.10
Weather	1.00	0.80	0.80	0.60	0.80	0.30	0.70
Total	100.00	100.00	100.00	100.00	100.00	100.00	100.00

contd...

contd...

January-December 2006	*% of News Time*						
Story Topic	*Aaj Tak*	*Sahara Samay*	*Star News*	*Zee News*	*NDTV India*	*DD News*	*Total*
Accident and Natural Disaster	1.20	2.20	1.10	0.80	0.90	1.30	1.30
Agriculture	0.10	0.60	0.00	0.10	0.20	1.60	0.50
Arts, Culture and Heritage	2.50	4.40	1.50	4.40	3.70	4.30	3.50
Business and Economy	7.30	2.30	2.10	1.90	4.30	17.40	6.30
Civic Issue	1.80	2.40	1.60	1.90	4.00	1.20	2.20
Crime	10.80	13.10	17.00	14.10	8.00	2.50	10.50
Corruption	0.30	0.20	0.40	0.10	0.60	0.00	0.30
Education	0.40	1.20	0.30	0.90	1.40	1.20	0.90
Election	0.20	0.80	0.20	0.40	0.70	1.20	0.60
Environment and Wildlife	0.10	0.90	0.10	0.40	0.40	0.90	0.50
Fashion and Life Style	0.50	1.60	0.60	1.00	0.40	0.00	0.70
Film and Entertainment	15.10	6.80	20.80	15.60	9.90	4.80	11.50
Health and Medicine	1.50	2.90	1.70	2.00	2.60	2.40	2.20
Human Interest	5.20	5.90	2.10	7.40	3.70	2.60	4.40
International Affairs	4.20	3.50	1.50	2.30	3.20	14.10	5.10
Law and Order	0.90	1.20	0.80	0.60	1.70	1.30	1.10
Legal	6.20	9.60	7.80	6.40	10.00	5.50	7.70
Media	0.30	0.10	0.00	0.10	0.00	0.80	0.20
National Politics	5.60	7.10	4.20	6.40	7.70	12.60	7.50
National Security and Defence	4.90	5.50	4.70	6.90	5.80	5.20	5.50
Others	0.60	0.80	1.90	1.00	1.70	1.90	1.30
Public Policy and Governance	0.40	1.00	0.60	0.60	1.80	2.70	1.30
Religion	0.90	1.60	0.20	2.00	1.00	0.60	1.00
Science and Technology	0.50	0.30	0.40	0.40	0.20	0.70	0.40
Sports	24.40	19.20	25.10	18.20	21.30	9.30	19.20
State Politics	3.40	4.60	2.70	3.80	4.50	2.90	3.70
Weather	0.60	0.50	0.20	0.20	0.20	0.50	0.40
Total	100.00	100.00	100.00	100.00	100.00	100.00	100.00

contd...

contd...

January-December 2007	*% of News Time*						
Story Topic	*Aaj Tak*	*Sahara Samay*	*Star News*	*Zee News*	*NDTV India*	*DD News*	*Total*
Accident and Natural Disaster	1.56	2.41	1.95	1.82	1.36	1.42	1.72
Agriculture	0.00	0.17	0.00	0.02	0.28	0.54	0.19
Arts, Culture and Heritage	0.39	0.50	0.43	0.70	0.49	1.35	0.69
Business and Economy	0.75	1.34	1.02	0.89	3.10	18.97	4.75
Civic Issue	0.44	1.16	0.74	1.05	1.96	1.13	1.12
Corruption	0.30	0.43	0.43	0.30	1.02	0.22	0.44
Crime	12.62	12.10	16.61	16.38	9.66	2.68	11.06
Education	0.20	0.67	0.09	0.58	0.70	1.51	0.69
Election	1.88	5.68	1.52	3.46	7.13	4.75	4.34
Environment and Wildlife	0.44	0.59	0.86	0.60	0.41	2.06	0.88
Fashion and Life Style	0.03	0.40	0.05	0.36	0.46	0.03	0.25
Film and Entertainment	23.43	10.95	32.03	18.15	12.51	5.39	15.97
Health and Medicine	0.44	0.76	0.18	1.38	0.97	1.07	0.85
Human Interest	8.26	8.68	6.43	11.88	6.57	5.44	7.69
International Affairs	6.89	4.71	5.51	4.97	5.16	15.36	7.54
Law and Order	3.07	8.04	2.42	2.11	3.86	1.42	3.58
Legal	3.26	6.09	3.90	5.02	8.27	4.29	5.12
Media	0.12	0.14	0.31	0.12	0.41	0.82	0.33
National Politics	2.42	5.66	1.20	2.56	6.84	5.02	4.25
National Security and Defence	2.43	4.00	1.84	3.80	4.19	4.54	3.53
Others	0.32	1.11	0.61	0.83	0.78	3.24	1.23
Public Policy and Governance	0.31	0.93	0.36	0.72	1.37	2.05	1.03
Religion	1.54	2.01	0.98	4.03	2.09	2.16	2.11
Science and Technology	0.44	0.39	0.34	1.34	0.31	0.83	0.68
Sports	26.59	17.23	18.67	14.19	15.54	10.75	16.99
State Politics	1.62	3.59	1.17	2.47	4.24	1.86	2.65
Weather	0.26	0.28	0.35	0.25	0.33	0.49	0.32
Total	100.00	100.00	100.00	100.00	100.00	100.00	100.00

Notes: 1. Figures are based on prime time (7-11 pm) coverage of 6 national news channels.

2. Figures are percentage of total news time of 6 national news channels.

3. News channels–Aaj Tak, DD News, NDTV India, Sahara Samay, Star News and Zee News.

Annexure Table A-4.1

Channel-wise TV News Content Trends 2008-2014

January-December 2008	*% of News Time*						
Story Topic	*Aaj Tak*	*DD News*	*Star News*	*Zee News*	*NDTV 24x7*	*CNN IBN*	*Total*
Accident and Natural Disaster	1.92	1.74	2.70	2.43	0.89	1.12	1.77
Agriculture	0.00	1.12	0.00	0.10	0.12	0.09	0.29
Arts, Culture and Heritage	0.20	1.70	0.02	0.32	0.90	0.18	0.62
Civic Issue	0.37	1.19	1.05	1.30	2.08	1.73	1.31
Corruption	0.32	0.05	0.38	0.59	0.26	0.22	0.29
Crime	5.46	0.87	7.94	8.80	2.77	3.72	4.61
Education	0.04	1.57	0.15	0.50	0.84	0.49	0.66
Environment and Wildlife	0.43	1.11	0.61	0.70	1.00	0.58	0.77
Fashion and Life Style	0.08	0.08	0.50	0.29	0.52	0.16	0.27
Film and Entertainment	24.36	2.14	25.79	10.61	8.69	13.50	13.44
Health and Medicine	0.29	1.78	0.43	1.48	1.16	0.69	1.01
Human Interest	3.96	0.30	4.01	3.70	1.57	2.37	2.48
International Affairs	7.31	13.95	5.27	8.40	11.73	10.13	9.77
Law and Order	2.91	1.92	2.47	3.46	3.82	3.59	2.98
Legal	4.31	1.96	4.05	5.20	3.63	4.65	3.83
Media	0.28	0.59	0.13	0.20	0.56	0.79	0.44
National Politics	4.68	5.31	5.08	7.46	8.38	7.72	6.42
National Security and Defence	10.40	5.71	9.61	13.01	10.00	8.93	9.35
Others	0.33	3.99	0.32	1.35	2.28	1.23	1.73
Public Policy and Governance	0.32	3.88	0.37	1.36	1.06	1.54	1.55
Religion	3.79	1.24	1.94	3.35	0.60	0.62	1.82
Science and Technology	0.42	1.28	0.46	2.27	3.97	0.62	1.53
Sports	23.01	20.89	20.31	14.85	21.50	24.66	20.97
Election	0.93	3.85	1.85	1.55	2.33	2.15	2.22
State Politics	1.47	0.85	1.99	2.46	2.04	2.63	1.85
Business and Economy	2.26	20.38	2.42	4.11	7.09	5.64	7.76
Weather	0.14	0.54	0.15	0.15	0.20	0.24	0.26
Total	100.00	100.00	100.00	100.00	100.00	100.00	100.00

contd...

contd...

January-December 2009	*% of News Time*						
Story Topic	*Aaj Tak*	*DD News*	*Star News*	*Zee News*	*NDTV 24x7*	*CNN IBN*	*Total*
Accident and Natural Disaster	2.55	1.67	3.49	3.78	1.70	2.14	2.48
Agriculture	0.04	0.56	0.06	0.11	0.08	0.15	0.18
Arts, Culture and Heritage	0.39	2.28	0.58	1.06	0.29	0.41	0.88
Business and Economy	2.10	18.81	2.97	3.47	2.98	5.58	6.59
Civic Issue	0.58	0.92	1.24	2.31	2.61	1.18	1.44
Corruption	0.48	0.39	1.11	2.38	1.31	0.70	1.00
Crime	5.14	0.71	8.19	11.69	3.43	2.40	4.86
Education	0.10	1.63	0.24	0.82	0.92	1.10	0.85
Environment and Wildlife	1.56	2.31	1.29	1.23	0.89	1.71	1.53
Fashion and Life Style	0.07	0.06	0.11	0.14	0.11	0.29	0.13
Film and Entertainment	20.54	1.94	12.42	6.61	13.65	7.84	10.13
Health and Medicine	2.06	1.59	1.02	1.74	2.06	2.75	1.87
Human Interest	2.86	1.38	2.18	2.60	2.63	1.23	2.09
International Affairs	13.95	12.98	11.84	12.09	10.46	12.90	12.38
Law and Order	1.32	1.01	2.34	2.19	2.68	2.85	2.04
Legal	0.66	1.28	1.73	2.58	2.27	3.00	1.91
Media	0.24	0.58	0.16	0.12	0.50	0.92	0.45
National Politics	4.73	7.46	6.42	8.09	7.00	9.68	7.27
National Security and Defence	4.54	3.74	4.10	9.93	3.47	5.19	4.98
Others	2.23	4.16	1.16	2.45	3.57	3.16	2.87
Public Policy and Governance	0.23	4.72	0.94	2.68	2.35	2.29	2.31
Religion	2.57	0.53	1.41	1.07	0.41	0.86	1.09
Science and Technology	0.59	0.63	0.40	1.88	0.92	1.33	0.93
Sports	19.61	17.47	20.54	4.90	17.97	13.99	16.03
Election	8.32	9.42	11.29	9.05	12.79	12.95	10.69
State Politics	1.95	1.07	2.21	4.22	2.45	3.01	2.40
Weather	0.60	0.71	0.56	0.81	0.51	0.38	0.59
Total	100.00	100.00	100.00	100.00	100.00	100.00	100.00

contd...

contd...

January-December 2010	*% of News Time*						
Story Topic	*Aaj Tak*	*DD News*	*Star News*	*Zee News*	*NDTV 24x7*	*CNN IBN*	*Total*
Accident and Natural Disaster	4.05	2.08	4.97	5.88	1.99	2.25	3.39
Agriculture	0.08	0.80	0.01	0.05	0.01	0.07	0.19
Arts, Culture and Heritage	0.25	1.13	0.95	0.61	0.11	0.80	0.65
Business and Economy	0.30	12.08	1.45	3.32	1.66	3.85	4.09
Civic Issue	2.19	0.53	1.90	2.24	5.35	1.40	2.24
Corruption	2.72	1.40	1.94	7.47	4.41	7.40	4.13
Crime	7.75	0.90	9.76	11.90	3.91	2.66	5.74
Education	0.25	0.92	0.25	0.13	0.53	0.78	0.51
Environment and Wildlife	0.97	1.34	1.45	0.97	0.69	2.26	1.29
Fashion and Life Style	0.16	0.05	0.06	0.07	0.79	0.63	0.31
Film and Entertainment	22.82	3.19	26.98	5.41	14.77	5.78	12.74
Health and Medicine	1.42	1.39	1.40	1.27	0.89	0.82	1.19
Human Interest	1.82	1.31	3.18	1.26	1.97	2.28	1.97
International Affairs	4.50	13.25	4.16	5.77	8.10	11.08	8.14
Law and Order	1.96	2.78	2.02	3.67	2.41	4.78	2.95
Legal	2.85	2.74	2.32	3.56	4.90	5.21	3.62
Media	0.23	0.78	0.17	0.05	1.54	0.68	0.62
National Politics	4.31	12.01	5.00	8.34	9.24	11.04	8.56
National Security and Defence	3.14	2.87	3.75	8.44	3.24	3.84	4.08
Others	8.02	6.48	1.23	7.26	2.59	3.28	4.73
Public Policy and Governance	1.06	7.75	1.74	5.10	3.92	5.01	4.26
Religion	3.21	1.05	1.19	1.22	0.52	0.49	1.23
Science and Technology	0.17	0.49	0.30	1.02	0.64	1.49	0.69
Sports	20.50	19.05	19.22	8.64	21.24	17.44	17.93
Election	0.35	1.35	1.73	0.27	0.47	0.86	0.87
State Politics	3.71	1.11	2.28	4.81	3.77	3.15	3.04
Weather	1.21	1.18	0.58	1.26	0.33	0.69	0.86
Total	100.00	100.00	100.00	100.00	100.00	100.00	100.00

contd...

contd...

January-December 2011	*% of News Time*						
Story Topic	*Aaj Tak*	*DD News*	*Star News*	*Zee News*	*NDTV 24x7*	*CNN IBN*	*Total*
Accident and Natural Disaster	2.99	1.63	3.26	3.71	1.44	1.16	2.27
Agriculture	0.01	0.30	0.02	0.09	0.03	0.05	0.09
Arts, Culture and Heritage	0.49	2.80	0.68	0.62	0.42	0.71	1.03
Business and Economy	1.43	13.07	2.08	2.31	2.20	3.39	4.47
Civic Issue	7.02	3.94	8.77	9.86	7.89	7.33	7.30
Corruption	3.92	4.26	6.03	7.19	9.08	5.36	5.94
Crime	6.75	1.46	8.27	11.19	3.24	2.18	5.16
Education	0.18	1.54	0.15	0.31	0.22	0.90	0.60
Environment and Wildlife	0.32	1.28	0.79	0.46	0.58	1.38	0.84
Fashion and Life Style	0.05	0.01	0.08	0.00	0.10	1.43	0.30
Film and Entertainment	14.76	3.45	10.90	2.87	17.70	9.65	9.72
Health and Medicine	1.01	1.32	0.94	1.37	0.82	0.58	1.00
Human Interest	4.70	2.99	2.45	2.09	3.41	1.03	2.74
International Affairs	7.70	13.24	7.00	6.75	8.47	11.06	9.29
Law and Order	0.72	0.71	1.36	1.25	1.30	1.14	1.07
Legal	1.69	2.40	1.81	3.36	2.75	3.68	2.64
Media	0.16	0.79	0.34	0.10	1.71	0.75	0.67
National Politics	11.02	9.57	13.85	14.98	9.96	19.74	13.15
National Security and Defence	4.02	2.95	3.35	6.24	2.40	3.82	3.72
Others	0.72	1.14	0.35	4.65	1.09	1.24	1.48
Public Policy and Governance	2.27	6.96	2.97	5.27	4.72	3.11	4.33
Religion	1.20	0.73	0.69	0.37	0.24	0.42	0.60
Science and Technology	0.43	0.81	0.24	0.60	0.19	1.25	0.61
Sports	23.21	16.18	20.21	7.74	16.43	13.21	16.09
Election	0.37	3.30	1.42	0.96	1.80	1.72	1.69
State Politics	2.39	2.51	1.77	5.21	1.64	3.68	2.84
Weather	0.48	0.67	0.23	0.45	0.16	0.05	0.34
Total	100.00	100.00	100.00	100.00	100.00	100.00	100.00

contd...

contd...

January-December 2012	*% of News Time*						
Story Topic	*Aaj Tak*	*DD News*	*Star News*	*Zee News*	*NDTV 24x7*	*CNN IBN*	*Total*
Accident and Natural Disaster	2.95	0.95	2.73	3.05	1.15	1.27	1.95
Agriculture	0.00	0.28	0.01	0.07	0.00	0.05	0.08
Arts, Culture and Heritage	0.52	1.83	0.46	0.77	0.17	0.96	0.83
Business and Economy	2.06	9.27	2.41	3.07	3.47	3.84	4.22
Civic Issue	5.15	3.17	5.40	7.92	6.06	6.05	5.55
Corruption	3.12	1.74	5.09	5.14	3.79	4.86	3.91
Crime	6.08	7.02	6.28	11.43	5.34	4.05	6.63
Education	0.06	1.61	0.23	0.29	0.40	0.91	0.63
Environment and Wildlife	0.11	0.92	0.58	0.39	0.74	1.02	0.65
Fashion and Life Style	0.09	0.05	0.00	0.03	0.13	0.80	0.20
Film and Entertainment	16.34	2.06	10.10	4.73	19.95	10.15	10.16
Health and Medicine	0.58	1.31	1.01	1.36	0.79	0.89	1.00
Human Interest	1.74	1.98	2.61	1.50	3.06	1.87	2.11
International Affairs	4.30	11.65	4.14	5.91	8.05	8.77	7.37
Law and Order	0.46	1.16	0.81	0.58	1.11	1.83	1.03
Legal	1.39	2.04	2.53	2.35	1.55	2.50	2.08
Media	0.08	1.08	0.22	0.18	0.62	0.52	0.48
National Politics	21.12	14.21	20.78	22.02	16.52	20.42	19.04
National Security and Defence	2.20	3.07	2.49	3.99	2.98	3.68	3.10
Others	1.30	1.69	0.85	1.65	1.34	0.90	1.29
Public Policy and Governance	0.69	6.38	2.42	2.74	1.87	3.06	3.01
Religion	0.55	0.35	0.39	0.39	0.08	0.17	0.32
Science and Technology	0.42	1.10	0.27	1.60	0.21	1.76	0.94
Sports	19.32	14.35	13.30	6.17	14.31	11.28	13.06
Election	6.05	8.51	10.96	8.34	4.24	5.33	7.23
State Politics	1.74	1.61	3.13	3.19	1.89	2.99	2.42
Weather	1.57	0.60	0.79	1.14	0.18	0.08	0.70
Total	100.00	100.00	100.00	100.00	100.00	100.00	100.00

contd...

contd...

January-December 2013	*% of News Time*						
Story Topic	*Aaj Tak*	*DD News*	*Star News*	*Zee News*	*NDTV 24x7*	*CNN IBN*	*Total*
Accident and Natural Disaster	5.68	3.45	4.47	3.95	2.79	3.06	3.80
Agriculture	0.01	0.18	0.01	0.00	0.05	0.02	0.05
Arts, Culture and Heritage	0.12	1.37	0.34	0.63	0.92	1.37	0.85
Business and Economy	0.97	7.16	2.99	1.32	2.51	3.84	3.34
Civic Issue	1.81	1.56	2.39	6.56	4.30	3.45	3.30
Corruption	2.99	1.71	2.62	3.51	4.43	3.98	3.21
Crime	10.79	6.05	9.41	14.25	5.88	5.55	8.31
Education	0.07	1.24	0.20	0.40	0.68	1.19	0.69
Environment and Wildlife	0.02	0.54	0.23	0.25	0.43	0.34	0.32
Fashion and Life Style	0.03	0.00	0.00	0.04	0.10	0.49	0.12
Film and Entertainment	10.99	2.11	11.75	11.51	15.85	7.29	9.58
Health and Medicine	0.40	1.04	1.03	1.64	0.99	1.23	1.06
Human Interest	0.94	1.32	1.41	3.75	3.20	2.29	2.15
International Affairs	7.37	15.49	5.11	6.83	8.18	8.25	8.83
Law and Order	1.39	2.10	1.13	1.20	0.94	1.87	1.47
Legal	1.76	3.86	3.21	2.69	2.75	3.97	3.12
Media	0.10	1.15	0.05	0.21	0.58	0.35	0.44
National Politics	21.69	18.84	27.28	16.19	17.89	22.81	20.74
National Security and Defence	3.35	3.65	2.93	4.07	3.05	3.95	3.52
Others	2.47	1.72	2.52	0.92	1.80	1.49	1.80
Public Policy and Governance	0.85	8.11	1.69	2.25	3.62	4.32	3.74
Religion	1.23	0.70	0.52	1.19	0.06	0.08	0.59
Science and Technology	0.14	0.90	0.15	0.76	0.24	0.93	0.55
Sports	15.47	6.44	7.59	8.63	11.63	11.16	10.04
Election	3.98	5.54	3.92	3.78	4.47	3.60	4.25
State Politics	4.13	3.45	6.57	2.60	2.53	2.96	3.64
Weather	1.28	0.33	0.48	0.87	0.14	0.18	0.50
Total	100.00	100.00	100.00	100.00	100.00	100.00	100.00

contd...

.contd...

January-December 2014	% of News Time						
Story Topic	Aaj Tak	DD News	ABP News	Zee News	CNN IBN	NDTV 24x7	Total
Accident and Natural Disaster	3.28	3.38	2.88	2.99	1.95	2.18	2.76
Agriculture	0.07	0.30	0.09	0.01	0.25	0.30	0.18
Arts,Culture and Heritage	0.60	2.02	0.59	1.24	0.58	1.41	1.13
Business and Economy	1.64	4.79	2.07	1.29	2.72	2.02	2.54
Civic Issue	1.31	1.23	1.38	3.05	2.76	1.79	1.89
Corruption	3.28	1.97	2.62	4.77	1.82	2.49	2.73
Crime	3.45	1.93	4.95	6.24	4.10	3.68	3.92
Education	0.58	1.79	0.93	1.95	1.29	2.10	1.48
Environment and Wildlife	0.69	1.00	0.53	0.60	0.62	0.93	0.75
Fashion and Life Style	0.03	0.01	0.00	0.14	0.00	0.44	0.11
Film and Entertainment	5.81	1.51	7.80	4.26	15.87	7.63	7.08
Health and Medicine	0.35	1.89	0.70	1.29	1.45	1.23	1.20
Human Interest	1.39	0.53	0.62	3.82	0.91	1.28	1.35
International Affairs	9.48	16.59	8.03	13.53	8.35	9.67	11.12
Law and Order	1.20	0.79	1.51	1.28	0.90	1.36	1.15
Legal	0.60	2.50	1.11	1.31	1.68	2.13	1.64
Media	0.11	1.90	0.11	0.24	0.22	0.24	0.53
National Politics	22.96	12.89	19.91	13.49	13.01	18.47	16.58
National Security and Defence	1.81	2.32	1.58	2.74	1.80	2.38	2.12
Others	0.57	1.96	0.82	1.88	0.85	0.99	1.20
Public Policy and Governance	2.12	8.76	2.51	5.16	3.11	4.22	4.52
Religion	1.01	0.44	0.94	1.78	0.12	0.07	0.66
Science and Technology	0.17	0.73	0.30	0.65	0.44	0.53	0.49
Sports	8.78	3.83	3.63	2.04	9.49	7.60	5.96
Election	22.10	20.75	27.96	20.29	22.09	20.78	22.18
State Politics	5.32	3.80	6.06	3.41	3.44	3.98	4.28
Weather	1.27	0.40	0.35	0.55	0.19	0.10	0.45
Total	100.00	100.00	100.00	100.00	100.00	100.00	100.00

Notes: 1. Figures are based on Prime Time (7-11 pm) Coverage of 6 national news channels.

2. Figures are percentage of total news time of 6 national news channels.

3. News channels–Aaj Tak, CNN IBN, DD News, NDTV 24x7, Star News/ABP News and Zee News.

Annexure Table A-5.1

Rate Your News Channels: Where Do They Stand?

(Alok Srivastava)

Television news channels' presence in India is growing at an unimaginable pace. With around 405 permitted television news channels in the country by January 2015, for a population of more than 1.2 billion, India is witnessing availability of a variety for countrymen, literate or illiterate. What is heartening is that television-deprived locations in India are decreasing day by day due to growing reach of television channels. As true for every aspect, expansion and reach of media has its pros and cons as well.

Alphabet	*Choice 1*	*Choice 2*	*Your CHOICE**
A.	Amiable	Arrogant	
B.	Bold	Biased	
C.	Critic	Copycat	
D.	Daring	Discreditable	
E.	Empathise	Egoistic	
F.	Factual	Fudge	
G.	Grilling	Goof-up	
H.	Humble	Horrifying	
I.	Intrinsic (Genuine)	Instigate	
J.	Justifiable	Judgmental	
K.	Kind	(feel as if) King maker	
L.	Legitimate	Laughable	
M.	Maturity	Malign/Mockery	
N.	Noticeable	Nuisance	
O.	Open	Overplay	
P.	Professional	Profit-making	
Q.	Quiet	Quarrelsome	
R.	Rational	Ridiculous	
S.	Sensible	Stupid	
T.	Trustworthy	Target	
U.	United	Uncalled for	
V.	Verifiable	Vindictive	
W.	Worthy	Wasteful	
X.	Xenodocile (nice/hospitable)	Xerox	
Y.	Yak (converse)	Yell	
Z.	Zeal	Zealous	
Total Score (A+Z)			

Note: * +1 for choice 1 and -1 for choice 2

Particularly in the recent times, given the competition among media houses, uncertainty looming high on the employment status of staff including news presenters/anchors in television has increased the race 'to be first' in sharing the news. In fact, the race is to present every event/activity more as sensational news rather than a piece of information. It is always welcome to present a news based on in-depth investigation of news, but should not be packaged every time with own analysis and judgment of the anchor/journalist or media house's stand of view. Why then does it often happen or that you get a feel when you see a news channel that anchor has a neutral stand, rather they create a layer of their own perception over the news item. Is it because the new presenters and editors feel that Indian citizens are immature to form an opinion on their own? In other words, do Indians lack the sense to analyse the right and wrong out of a news-worthy event or activity?

TV News Media Assessment Score: Based on the observation of good and bad news presentation of news articles, features and reports in both electronic and print media, I would like to draw the image of Indian television news channels using 26 alphabets of English language. Two choices are given for each alphabet and the reader has to select one, as per her/his observation about the television news channels. Undoubtedly, one has positive connotation while the other has negative reflection on the channel's presentation. The negative connotation has a score of -1, while each positive opinion about television news channel gives the channel a score of +1.

This assessment test by viewer of television news channel will reflect upon its credibility in the eyes of the viewers of news channels. With little adaptation and contextualisation, the assessment can be used for newspapers as well as any institution whether, parliament/politicians, executives/bureaucrats/public services or NGOs/civil society groups, the key pillars of democracy.

How to Calculate:

The final score will thus reflect on the quality of television news channels, based on the score attained.

Score Card

Rating	*Score*	*Scoring method*
Excellent	26-25	If for all 25-26 alphabets, positive words are selected
Good	16-22	If for 21-24 alphabets, positive words are selected and rest negative
Average	12-14	If for 19-20 alphabets, positive words are selected and rest negative
Poor	2-10	If for 14-18 alphabets, positive words are selected and rest negative
Worst/	0 or less	If for only 13 alphabets, positive words are selected and for remaining 13 alphabets negative